EAGLES OF THE LUFTWAFFE: FOCKE-WULF FW 190 A, F AND G

DAN SHARP

TEMPEST BOOKS

For Steve Coates.

First published in Great Britain in 2021
by Tempest Books
an imprint of Mortons Books Ltd.
Media Centre
Morton Way
Horncastle LN9 6JR
www.mortonsbooks.co.uk

ISBN 978 1 911658 05 4

Typeset by S4Carlisle Publishing Services
Printed and bound in Great Britain

Contents

Chapter 1

Introduction

When 33-year-old aircraft designer and pilot Kurt Tank left Bayerische Flugzeugwerke (BFW) in Augsburg to join Focke-Wulf as chief designer on 1 November 1931, the Bremen-based company employed a total of just 150 people, including sales staff.

The firm had been established by engineer Henrich Focke, on 23 October 1923, and his business partner, Georg Wulf, who became the company's test pilot. The latter was killed testing the radical tail-first Focke-Wulf F.19 Ente on 29 September 1927, but the company nevertheless kept his name for the next 18 years.

Focke himself, despite also having his name on the company's letterheads, was not Focke-Wulf's owner but held the position of technical director. His work was effectively bankrolled by a group of businessmen, led by wealthy aviation enthusiast Dr Ludwig Roselius, founder and owner of Bremen-based Kaffee HAG—a successful company that had pioneered the world's first commercial decaffeination process.

As company chairman, Roselius became dissatisfied with Focke's performance—while his aircraft were acceptable they weren't outstanding. He saw an opportunity to dramatically change the company's fortunes in 1931, when the much larger but near-bankrupt Albatros concern reached the point of collapse.

The acquisition of Albatros brought with it large new production facilities and experienced engineers who could design and build cutting-edge modern aircraft. Tank, who had made a name for himself with Rohrbach before joining Willy Messerschmitt at BFW, was

ABOVE: Aircraft such as the Focke-Wulf A 17 Möwe airliner helped to establish the company during the late 1920s.

ABOVE: Designer Kurt Tank joined Focke-Wulf in November 1931, shortly after the firm's merger with Albatros, and two years later became its technical director.

brought in to lead Focke-Wulf's newly expanded team.

After assessing the existing products of both Focke-Wulf and Albatros, Tank presented his plan for the future of the company's aircraft to the directors in 1933—now they would be built entirely of metal, rather than wood, with a focus on high performance. The company asked the German government to indicate whether aircraft of this type would be ordered and was given assurances that they would. Tank was duly promoted to technical director in place of Focke, who, while he remained on the company's board, had little further input on the company's design and production of fixed-wing aircraft.

Tank's first new design was the Fw 44 Stieglitz (Goldfinch) trainer—a biplane with two open cockpits, each with a set of instruments and flight controls. It was powered by an air-cooled 150hp Siemens-Halske Sh 14a radial engine. Although the layout was established by Tank, the detailed design was by Ludwig Mittelhüber, an engineer who had followed Tank from Messerschmitt. It was a process that was to become a familiar part of the Focke-Wulf design ethos—Tank would approve a layout and an engine before his team did the rest.

The Fw 44 first flew in August 1932 and after early problems with oscillation were cured, orders started to come in. The Fw 44 A was in production by the end of the year, and the improved Fw 44 B appeared in 1933, with large-scale production commencing in 1934. It was Focke-Wulf's first mass-produced aircraft, and 1900-3000 examples were built, many by subcontractors, including AGO, Bücker and Siebel and by licensed builders in Austria, Argentina, Bulgaria, Brazil and Sweden. It was also sold to Bolivia, Chile, China, Czechoslovakia, Finland, Romania and Switzerland.

As the Stieglitz became increasingly successful, Tank persuaded his fellow directors that some of the newly generated proceeds should be reinvested in the company. He then set about creating the next range of Focke-Wulf aircraft, just as the government was laying out its plans to revive the German air force. This had been disbanded after the First World War under the provisions of the Treaty of Versailles by May 1920, leaving the country without any form of military aviation.

There were still thousands of pilots and aviation enthusiasts, however, who were unwilling to accept this ban, and military training took place in secret at many civil aviation schools throughout the 1920s.

When Adolf Hitler formed the new Nazi government in January 1933, one of his first acts was to formalise the creation of a new air force—in direct contravention of the restrictions imposed by the Allies. Former fighter ace Hermann Göring became the country's first post-war commissioner for aviation, with Lufthansa director Erhard Milch as his deputy. All former covert military aviation

ABOVE: The Fw 44's success helped to establish Focke-Wulf as a major player in Germany's burgeoning aircraft industry.

organisations were merged into one body on 15 May 1933, and Milch, with the newly formed Reichsluftfahrtministerium (RLM), set about obtaining the aircraft that were needed to create a true Luftwaffe.

Requirements were drawn up for types to fill a multitude of roles, including single-seat advanced trainer, multirole transport, medium bomber, light bomber, two-seat heavy fighter and single-seat fighter. Invitations to tender were then sent out to Germany's burgeoning aviation industry—including Focke-Wulf.

The company was asked to submit designs for the single-seat trainer alongside Arado, Heinkel and Henschel, and the result was the Fw 56 Stösser (Goshawk)—a slender monoplane powered by a 240hp Argus As 10 C engine. Around 1000 examples were built. A tender for the two-seat heavy fighter issued in June 1934 produced the Fw 57, competing against BFW's Bf 110 and Henschel's Hs 124. The Fw 57 made its first flight in October 1936, but the type was far too heavy and cumbersome in comparison with the 110. It had been cancelled in favour of the latter by April 1937, even before the second and third prototypes flew.

The requirement for a multirole aircraft saw the twin-engined Fw 58 Weihe (Harrier) enter full production, with more than 1350 examples being made—a civilian Fw 58 coded D-ALEX becoming Tank's personal aircraft.

Lastly, there was the most prestigious competition of all, that which would produce Germany's mainstay front-line single-seat fighter aircraft. Göring sent letters out to BFW, Arado and Heinkel in December 1933 asking that work be commenced on a 'high speed courier aircraft' immediately, while a formal request for fighter designs was sent out in February 1934.

Although it had not been invited to tender, towards the end of February Focke-Wulf's designers drew up four different Verfolgungseinziter or 'single seat pursuit' designs under

ABOVE: The heavy two-seater twin-engine Focke-Wulf Fw 57 fighter-bomber competed against Willy Messerschmitt's Bf 110 and lost.

ABOVE: Kurt Tank's second great success at Focke-Wulf was the Fw 56 Stösser single-seat advanced trainer. More than 1000 were built.

the project designation 77810B. Each was powered by a single liquid-cooled inline V12 BMW XV, producing 621hp at 3500m and had a wingspan of 12m.

The first design had a braced low wing and fixed undercarriage, the second a parasol wing with fixed undercarriage, the third a braced low wing with forward sweep and retractable undercarriage, and, lastly, a cantilever low wing with retractable undercarriage. Take-off weight for the first three was 1700kg, with a wing area of 17m^2, while for the cantilever wing type it was 1752kg and 17.5m^2.

The maximum speed of the parasol wing type was 412km/h at 4000m, 414km/h for

ABOVE: Operated in a range of different roles, the Fw 58 was a rugged and modern aeroplane. This is Tank's personal Fw 58, D-ALEX.

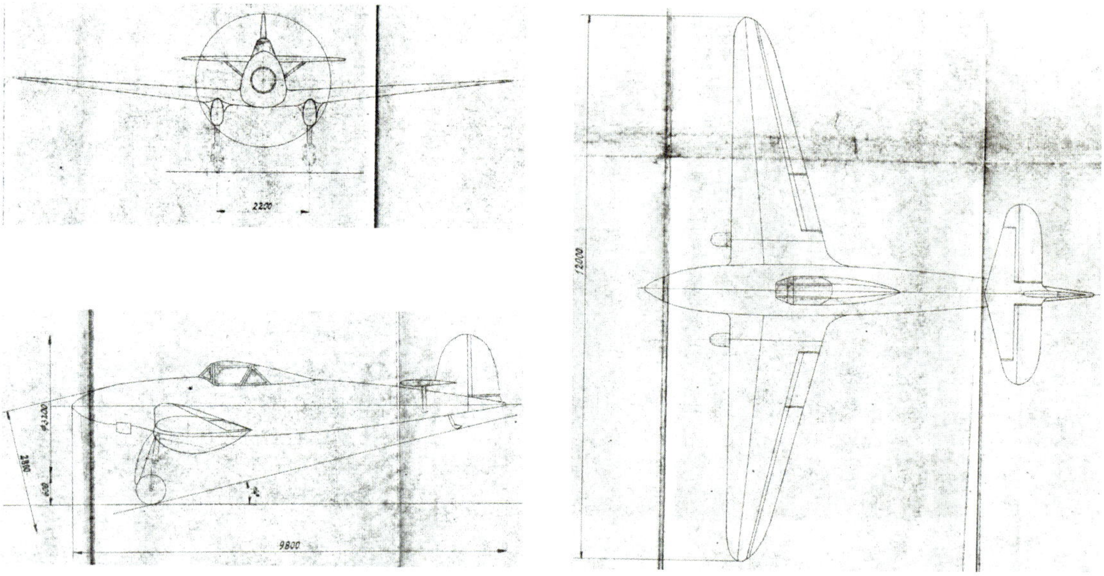

ABOVE: One of four alternative configurations for the Fw 159. History might have been different had Focke-Wulf chosen to pit its long-wing monoplane design with retractable undercarriage and bubble canopy against the Bf 109.

the two braced low-wing types, and the cantilever type was superior at 430km/h. The company report states:

> "The aerodynamic quality of the first three designs is about the same, whereas the cantilever low-wing type is somewhat better, because of the partially retractable landing gear (full retraction into the wing isn't possible). Frontal drag is reduced, but the drag of the wing is increased, because the wing had to be thickened for stability reasons."

The cantilever type's superior performance, it was stated, could be attributed solely to its retractable undercarriage.

All four designs could be expected to have a similar rate of turn, but pilot visibility was significantly better in the parasol winged type, with the forward swept design being second best, the standard braced low-wing type third and the cantilever low-wing type worst.

The report's anonymous author then notes:

> "For the envisaged purpose, interception of the enemy at great heights, especially important is the view slanting forward and downwards. Here the parasol winged type without doubt is superior to all other designs. The braced low wing with forward sweep only gives a partial view downwards at the level of the fuselage, which already is blocked in the standard braced low wing type, whereas the cantilever low wing type offers the least view.
>
> "When taking into account that usually the aircraft flies throttled back when waiting for the enemy, to save power and fuel, so the differences in the pilot's view become even more favourable. A low wing aircraft has to turn more often to achieve the same field of view as the parasol wing. Turning means loss of power and speed.
>
> "Preference should be given to the parasol wing type, because it's superior with regard to pilot visibility and hardly inferior with regard to flight performance compared to the low wing designs."

It was judged that loiter time at high altitude was essential so that a fighter could always be sure of attacking from above an opponent. And with this, Focke-Wulf's first modern fighter design—with cantilever low wing and retractable undercarriage—was dismissed in favour of a parasol wing design similar to, but not the same as, that of the Fw 56 Stösser.

FW 159

Focke-Wulf was given the opportunity to enter the fighter competition in September 1934, and the parasol wing design received the RLM number Fw 159, because Heinkel had already used 59. It was also given a novel undercarriage arrangement, where the mainwheels and legs folded up into the forward fuselage—alleviating the performance-degrading drag identified during the design phase. It had an enclosed cockpit with a sliding hood and two machine guns mounted on the nose above its Jumo 210 B engine (known initially as the Jumo 10).

RLM development charts for February 1935 show that the Fw 159 V1 was expected to make its first flight on September 1 that year, but by May the date had slipped to December 1. And at this point, while two Ar

ABOVE: Registered as D-IUPY, the Fw 159 V3 shows off its spindly undercarriage. The Fw 159's parasol wing was chosen for improved pilot visibility—despite its detrimental effect on overall performance.

80s, two Bf 109s and two He 112s were on order, Focke-Wulf appears to have been contracted for only one Fw 159.

A mock-up was completed in June 1935, and by November two Fw 159 prototypes were on order plus three 0-series pre-production aircraft—where the other three firms had orders for a trio of prototypes and seven 0-series machines. The date of the Fw 159's anticipated first flight had by now been moved to January 1936.

However, in the end the Fw 159 V1 first flew on 29 November 1935, with company test pilot Wolfgang Stein at the controls. The undercarriage was retracted after take-off, but after 30 minutes of flying, although they would extend, the oleo legs would not lock into place.

Stein tried to make them lock by putting the aircraft through a series of manoeuvres, but nothing worked, so he burned up as much fuel as possible before coming in to land with the gear unlocked. It collapsed on touch-down, and the aircraft somersaulted twice before coming to rest on its back. Although the aircraft was wrecked, Stein walked away with just bruises.

It was determined that the undercarriage had failed because Focke-Wulf's engineers had incorrectly calculated the amount of drag acting on the oleo legs—resulting in the hydraulic cylinder meant to lock the legs being insufficiently powerful. The second Fw 159 prototype, the V2, was therefore fitted with a more powerful cylinder.

Meanwhile, the first flight of the Bf 109 had taken place on 29 May 1935—albeit fitted with a British Rolls-Royce Kestrel VI engine because the company had been unable to obtain a Jumo 210. The Ar 80 had also flown with a Kestrel, and the He 112 was delayed.

As the year wore on, further tests were carried out, and a ready supply of Jumo 210 engines became available. The He 112 first flew in September with a Kestrel engine and then in November with a Jumo. Luftwaffe acceptance trials of the four designs finally began in late 1935 at Rechlin. The low-wing monoplane Ar 80 with its drag-inducing fixed undercarriage was judged to be the worst of the

ABOVE: During the autumn of 1935, Focke-Wulf's latest products were lined up for inspection during a company rally. From the left are an Fw 61 V1, Fw 44, Fw 56 V2, Fw 159 V1 and Fw 58 A-0.

four, but the He 112 proved to be a tougher opponent for the Fw 159. Designed by twin brothers Walter and Siegfried Günter, it was based on the world record-breaking He 70 fast mail carrier aeroplane and drawn up with a BMW radial engine in mind as Projekt 1015.

Performance was unremarkable to begin with, until the brothers realised that a smaller, thinner wing would result in a significant reduction in drag. With this problem cured, the He 112 was quickly chosen as the front runner in the competition. Finally, there was the Bf 109, which quickly demonstrated that its lightweight design gave it an unsurpassed level of performance.

On 1 January 1936, the RLM reported that the Ar 80 would not be built in series and was no longer an option for procurement—but the Fw 159 was now on a par with both the He 112 and the Bf 109 with three prototypes and seven 0-series aircraft on order.

Four months later, the Fw 159 V1 was still undergoing repairs, and the V2 was expected to make its first flight in May 1936. The Bf 109 V1, on the other hand, had been undergoing trials at a Luftwaffe test station since October 1935, and the 0-series order had been increased to 10 aircraft. The He 112 V1 had been undergoing tests since December 1935, and its 0-series order had risen to 12 aircraft.

The picture had changed again by July 1936. Both the Fw 159 V1 and the V2 were now undergoing repairs, the latter evidently flying for the first time in February but suffering a similar fate to the V1. Yet the Fw 159 A-0 series order had gone up to match Messerschmitt at 10 aircraft plus three prototypes—although the first three Bf 109s were now all being flight-tested. At this point there were 16 He 112s in progress—eight prototypes and eight 0-series aircraft, the first three also being flight-tested.

Remarkably, though, Focke-Wulf now had a new design on the RLM's books—the Fw 259—which was described as a Frontjäger rather than a Verfolgungs-Jagdeinsizter. Details on this design are scant (it was evidently outlined in Focke-Wulf Baubeschreibung Nr. 118 of 6 May 1936, of which no copies are known to survive) but it appears to have been effectively an Fw 159 fitted with a DB 600 engine, rather than the Jumo 210 B. Four prototypes and seven 0-series aircraft had apparently been commissioned by the RLM in March 1936, and a mock-up was due for completion in October.

By October the engine specified for the Fw 259 had been switched to the DB 601, but the RLM noted that a decision was still being made about whether to build a pre-production series. It was also noted that work on the Fw 159 continued to be delayed by accidents and vibration testing.

The Bf 109 V4 to V13 were being readied to join the Luftwaffe's test programme and two further He 112s had been ordered, making a total of 18.

Incredibly, the Fw 259 was still on order by April 1937, based on an updated description of 30 September 1936—although just four prototypes were to be built with series production cancelled because the type was 'not very interesting'. The Fw 159 too had been cancelled after the construction of three prototypes, Werk-Nr. 1963, 1964 and 1965.

Its problematic undercarriage was a fatal flaw, but its overall layout also made it appear ungainly and dated. Focke-Wulf Oberingenieur Heinz Conradis would later claim that the Fw 159's downfall was its development, at the behest of the RLM, as a dual role fighter and close reconnaissance aircraft—hence the emphasis on good downward visibility at the expense of performance.

In 1937, the third Fw 159 prototype was re-engined with a more powerful Jumo 210 G, enabling it to finally meet the original competition requirement of 250mph. The early prototypes had only managed 239mph. But again, this work went no further.

ABOVE: The second Focke-Wulf Fw 159 in flight. The type offered excellent visibility – at the expense of performance.

ABOVE: Another view of the Fw 159 V3, with its engine access hatches open. Note the stirrup step, which would become a feature of the Fw 190.

FW 187

While all this had been going on, Focke-Wulf had been hard at work on yet another fighter—a single seater but with two engines. The RLM development charts for 1 November 1935 and 1 January 1936 show a 'Verfolgungsjagd-einsitzer—2 Mot. Projekt FW' that was commissioned during February 1935. Then the chart for April 1936 shows that a mock-up of what was now called the Fw 187 was completed in January.

The Fw 187, described as a '2 mot. V. J.', appears below the other single seat fighter designs and is shown as being equipped with two Jumo 210 engines. An Fw 187 V1 is due to make its first flight in October 1936, followed by commencement of testing in February 1937, and a listing for a pre-production series, though there is a question mark where the number of aircraft ordered should be.

The Fw 187 was light and streamlined, unlike the unwieldy Fw 57, and unlike the Fw 159, it featured a very simply and dependable undercarriage. The main wheels retracted straight backwards into capacious nacelles behind the engines, and the tailwheel was also retractable. There were split flaps to make landing easier, and the fuselage was extremely narrow—so narrow, in fact, that there was no room on the cockpit dashboard for the engine gauges, which had to be placed on the sides of the engine nacelles facing the pilot so he could see them through the glass canopy.

By July the projected flight date for the V1 had shifted to December 1936, but there were now three prototypes and seven 0-series aircraft on order. Only the V1 was to be powered by a Jumo 210 D—the others were to feature the Jumo 210 G.

October saw the A-0 series increased to 11 aircraft, but in April 1937—as the Fw 159 and Fw 259 were being cancelled—it was noted that although the Fw 187 pre-production series was still planned, a decision about further work on the type would depend on the result of tests. The V1 took to the air for the first time on 10 April 1937 and in October it was stated that procurement of the Fw 187 would be decided following comparative tests against the Bf 109 and Bf 110.

The Fw 187 offered outstanding high-speed performance and excellent visibility, but it was lightly armed and lacked the ability to perform tight turns. The RLM initially declined to sanction further development of the type due to its weight—as much as two Bf 109s—and the fact that with two engines it would require twice as much maintenance.

When Ernst Udet took over from von Richthofen as the Technisches Amt's chief of development, he was impressed by the Fw 187's speed but somewhat less thrilled

ABOVE: Focke-Wulf came close to success with its slender Fw 187 twin-engine fighter design—producing a short run of pre-production aircraft.

ABOVE: The Fw 187 V3 which was later destroyed in a crash following an engine fire.

by what he regarded as its lack of manoeuvrability. Nevertheless, it was suggested that Tank could redesign the aircraft as a two-seat heavy fighter.

Tank therefore converted two of the prototypes, V3 and V4, by extending their fuselages. Second cockpits were installed, and fuel tanks were moved from the wings to the fuselage, allowing the Fw 187's flaps to be extended all the way along the wings.

The Fw 187 V1 was lost when its pilot, Paul Bauer, tried to pull a loop at low altitude. The aircraft lost too much speed and entered a flat spin at the apex of the loop, breaking apart when it hit the ground seconds later.

Despite this setback, the RLM issued a contract for two more two-seater prototypes—V5 and V6. The V6 finally saw the installation of the engines Tank had wanted all along, a pair of DB 600 As generating 1050hp each. During tests Fw 187 V6 was able to reach a top speed of 635km/h (394mph). The RLM gave Focke-Wulf a further contract for three pre-production aircraft—Fw 187 A-01 to Fw 187 A-03.

An RLM report of 3 September 1938 noted that "the following important aircraft types are still in V-pattern [prototype stage]. 0-series under construction. The decision about further procurement or introduction is still open". The types were:

> "Do 217 medium bomber and He 119 light bomber (introduction not yet planned); Bf 209 light fighter and He 100 light fighter (procurement except 0-series is so far not intended, since the continuous further development of the Bf 109 is more advantageous for the troops); Fw 190 light fighter with double star motor; Fw 187 two-seater fighter with heavy weapons and short range."

The Fw 187 never entered full production, and the remaining prototypes and pre-production aircraft were used to form a factory defence unit for Focke-Wulf's factories. The RLM note hints that all was not entirely well with the Bf 109—it was better than the Bf 209 (a fighter version of Messerschmitt's world air speed record attempt aircraft) and the He 112-derived He 100 only because it was easier to keep going with it than to switch to one of these other types.

There was growing concern within the RLM that the Bf 109 might not be sufficient to deal with the growing threat presented by the likes of Supermarine's Spitfire in Britain. It was also considered that most other countries had one or more different single-seat fighter designs operating in tandem and that Germany might do well to have its own *zweites eise im feuer* or 'second iron in the fire'.

Focke-Wulf had unsuccessfully developed three fighters to prototype stage and was clearly capable of coming up with innovative designs. Consequently, Tank had been approached by the RLM with an invitation to submit designs for an entirely new single-seat fighter—the Focke-Wulf Fw 190.

ABOVE: Fw 187 viewed from below. Note the instruments mounted on the engine nacelle.

Chapter 2

Early Development

When Willy Messerschmitt created the Bf 109 in 1934, there was very little else in the world to match its simple yet highly efficient design. It wasn't perfect, but it surpassed its contemporaries in almost every respect. By the time Kurt Tank and his team came to design the Fw 190 in 1938, the Bf 109 had seen action in the Spanish Civil War, and its imperfections had become readily apparent.

The Germans had also become increasingly concerned about the British Supermarine Spitfire. It was feared, with some justification, that this advanced fighter was already able to outperform the Bf 109.

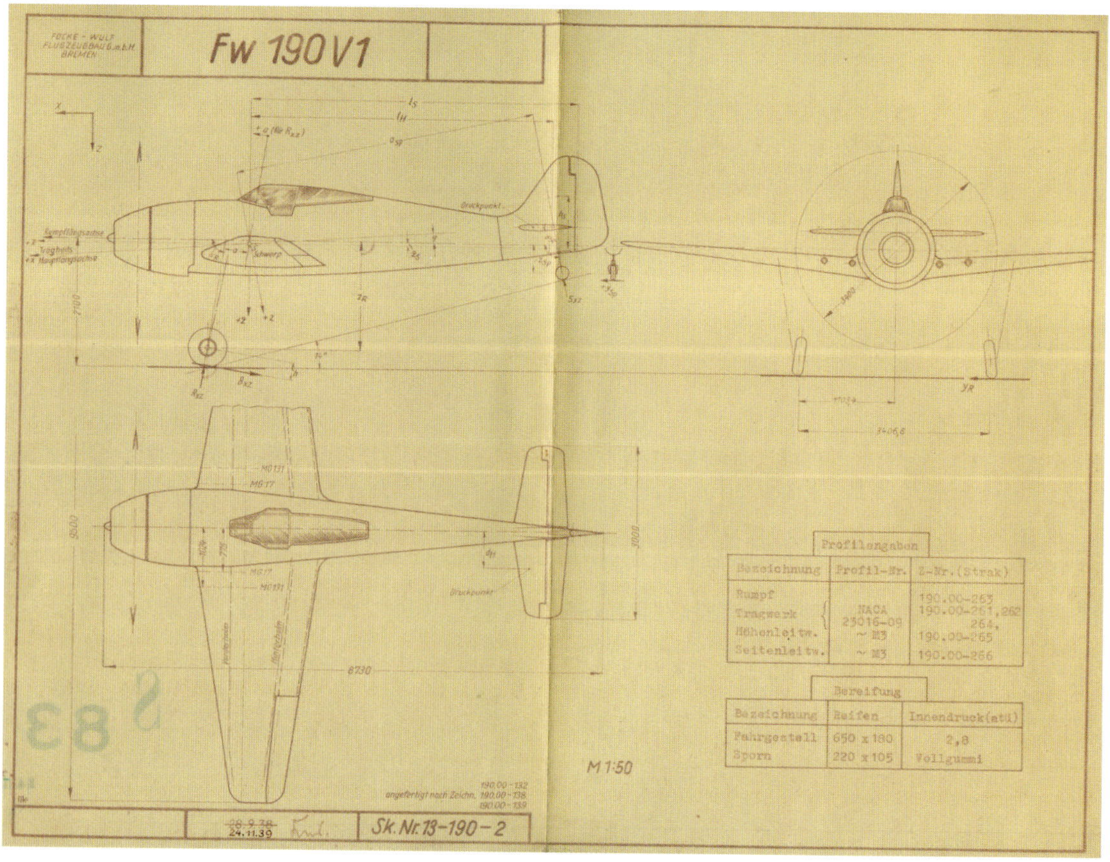

ABOVE: A 1939 reprint of an Fw 190 V1 drawing of 28 September 1938, showing the original fuselage and cockpit design.

Therefore, Focke-Wulf set out to develop an aeroplane that would not only address the Bf 109's flaws but also have a reasonable chance of besting the Spitfire—a tall order. It helped that the company was given leave to examine production Bf 109 machines up close and in detail before getting started.

It occurred to Tank that the Bf 109 and Spitfire were like racehorses—fast but requiring delicate handling to extract their best performance. Having served as a cavalry officer during the First World War, he decided that his new fighter needed to be a warhorse instead—fast but also rugged, easy to maintain, able to soak up punishment and capable of carrying heavy loads.

The Fw 190 would be tough and dependable, but it would also have to be able to keep up with the 'racehorses' where it mattered. The airframe would be sturdy enough to carry heavier weapons but not so heavy that it became slow and unwieldy. Good all-round visibility was also vital. The Bf 109's cockpit canopy had heavy frames, and the rearward view was less than satisfactory, so Tank's team came up with a sloping frameless canopy for improved visibility.

For the power plant, BMW's air-cooled 14-cylinder 1500hp fuel-injected radial 139 engine was chosen. While it was certainly true that an air-cooled engine could soak up more battle damage without failing than a liquid-cooled unit, which might rapidly run dry and seize, the main reason for picking the 139 was availability. Daimler-Benz's DB 600 series was already needed for the Bf 109, Bf 110 and Me 210, not to mention the He 177 and Me 261 (in DB 606 linked engine form).

The BMW 139 was designed with two rows of seven cylinders positioned back to back. Compared with an inline design such as the DB 601, it had a higher power to weight ratio but at the cost of generating an enormous amount of heat in a small area.

Tank himself said:

> "So the air-cooled radial engine was fitted to the Fw 190. When the fighter went into action the resilience of this type of power plant was proved again and again. There were several occasions when these fighters returned home and made normal landings, having had whole cylinders shot away. Once its cooling system had been pierced and the liquid allowed to drain away, the running life of the equivalent liquid-cooled engine would have been about three minutes."

Designs were submitted to the RLM, and Focke-Wulf was given an order to proceed with the construction of prototypes.

In working out how to build the Fw 190, Tank's team decided that simplicity was critical. The engine was attached directly to the monocoque fuselage, avoiding the need for engine mounts, and two removable self-sealing fuel tanks were fitted directly beneath the pilot.

The smaller (232-litre) tank was below the pilot's legs, and the larger (292 litre) tank was directly behind it under and behind his seat. This gave the Fw 190 more than twice the fuel capacity of the Bf 109, which could only carry 250 litres internally.

The wings, featuring split flaps, were built as a separate piece, and a series of ridges and corresponding grooves allowed them to be quickly moved into the correct position on the fuselage when fitted. After the trouble caused by the hydraulically operated undercarriage on the Fw 159, the Fw 190 used a system of cables that were electrically wound in or out on drums to raise and lower its main and tail wheels. The only exceptions were the first two prototypes, which both had hydraulic systems.

The Bf 109 had a narrow track undercarriage, where the wheels retracted outwards into the wings, restricting what weapons could be fitted there. In contrast, the Fw 190 had a wide track, and the wheels retracted inwards under the fuselage, reducing intrusion into the wings and freeing up space.

The first armament arrangement to be fitted was two machine guns and two cannons—a 7.9mm MG 17 with 800 rounds and a 20mm MG 151 with 160 rounds in each wing, close to the fuselage.

Ease of maintenance was another consideration in the Fw 190's design. Components that would require frequent servicing were positioned within easy reach, and large access panels were provided.

Climbing aboard the fighter, which stood nearly 4m tall at its highest point, compared with the Bf 109's 2.6m, was made easier with a retractable step on the lower edge of the fuselage on the port side, aft of the wing root. Then there was a spring-loaded handhold and a further step.

Inside the cockpit, the seat was semi-reclined and vertically adjustable over a range of 4in. The instruments were deliberately laid out in a logical way, with the most commonly used control closest to hand. A 1000W generator provided a 24V power supply for internal systems.

The BMW 139 drove a three-bladed Vereingite Deutsche Metallwerke (VDM) electro-hydraulic variable pitch 3.4m diameter propeller. Over this was fitted a large Doppelhaube ducted spinner intended to reduce drag.

A wooden mock-up was made during the autumn of 1938, and then work was started on the prototype, Fw 190 V1. Its first flight was on 1 June 1939, and test pilot Hans Sander recalled:

"For the first flight, I wore only a thin flying suit over my normal underwear, socks, ordinary shoes, and a flying helmet with my oxygen mask hanging loose, yet soon after take-off I began to sweat profusely.

"The rear of the engine was hard up against the front wall of the cockpit, and my feet and rudder pedals were either side of the engine accessories. The temperature in the cockpit rose to 55°C. I felt as though I was sitting with my feet in the fire. The heat was bearable but ever since I have had some sympathy for a steak on a grill."

ABOVE: A wooden model of the Fw 190 V1 built in 1938. It is marked up to show how the aircraft itself will be constructed.

LEFT: The Fw 190 V1 with Doppelhaube spinner fitted over its VDM propeller. Based on wind tunnel tests, it was calculated that the large ducted spinner would improve the aircraft's top speed by 25mph. However, in reality, it caused too much drag.

ABOVE: The stirrup step remains unretracted in this side view of an engine run-up test. At this stage the aircraft has not been painted and remains in bare metal finish.

Sander also had to put his oxygen mask on because engine exhaust fumes were beginning to leak through the improperly sealed edges of the canopy. Despite these problems, the test was deemed a success. The Fw 190 V1, given the civil registration D-OPZE, was shown to Adolf Hitler, Hermann Göring, Ernst Udet and Erhard Milch just over a month later, on 3 July 1939.

At this stage it had no armament fitted, and there was a problem with the V1's hydraulic undercarriage up-lock mechanism. The landing gear would rise and lock after take-off, but then, during aerial manoeuvres, the oleo legs would become unlocked and sag down. This was fixed by fitting a new, stronger mechanism based on a bomb release shackle.

Cooling problems persisted as testing continued, and BMW identified the Doppelhaube spinner as the problem, but Focke-Wulf opted to keep it. Reichlin experimental centre test pilot Heinrich Beauvais visited Focke-Wulf on 31 October 1939 to assess D-OPZE, now re-registered as FO+LY.

ABOVE: With its civil registration, D-OPZE, visible on the underside of its wings, Fw 190 V1 comes in to land.

ABOVE: Chief of the RLM's technical office Ernst Udet, centre, discusses the Fw 190 with his chief engineer, Rulof Lucht, left, a former naval aviator, and the chief test pilot of the Rechlin test centre, Carl Francke, right.

He later wrote:

"We instinctively preferred the Fw 190 over the Bf 109 from the very start. The Fw 190's control forces are significantly lower at high speeds, and its rate of roll is markedly greater."Furthermore, its wide-track undercarriage and the superior rigidity of its airframe are highly thought of, especially in belly-landings. The view to the rear is superior, and its BMW radial engine is less vulnerable to enemy fire. There was a tendency to disbelieve its inferiority in turning. Our report states: "It has yet to be determined whether the Fw 190 turns tighter than the Bf 109." In my opinion this should be viewed as misleading."It is true that turning radii were not measured, but that did not really matter. What did matter was turning times, and in this respect the Bf 109 was clearly superior. However, it needed barely four seconds to perform a complete roll, compared to five seconds for the Bf 109."

On the same day the Fw 190 V2, FO+LZ, made its first flight with machine guns, cannon, FuG VII radio and Revi C/12C gunsight fitted. Around this time the Fw 190 was given its Focke-Wulf bird name; following on from the tradition established by the Stieglitz, Stösser, Weihe and the rest, it was called Würger (Shrike).

Two months later, after suffering from the same overheating problems of the V1 (now coded FO+LY), it also had a new 10-bladed cooling fan fitted beneath its spinner. This helped a little but failed to cure the problem. BMW persisted with its claim that the spinner was the problem and Focke-Wulf finally relented. Comparative tests were conducted in January 1940 using the two prototypes, with Fw 190 V2 retaining its Doppelhaube, while V1's was removed and replaced with a NACA-style cowling.

ABOVE: Fitted with a conventional BMW-designed NACA-style cowling, Fw 190 V1 no longer suffered additional drag from its Doppelhaube spinner but was still prone to overheating.

These trials revealed that the spinner was actually slowing the aircraft down by about 12mph. Focke-Wulf had failed to account for the inch-wide gap between the spinner and the engine cowling, which caused air to be sucked through the propeller hub, causing drag.

The Doppelhaube concept was scrapped, and all future Fw 190s had a National Advisory Committee for Aeronautics (NACA)-style cowling instead. With this in place, the V2 was demonstrated for Göring, and an order for 40 pre-production aircraft, known as the Fw 190 A-0, followed. The V2 was now re-registered as RM+CB but was damaged in an accident on 2 March 1940, when it flipped over onto its back while taxiing. Repaired, it was used for weapons trials starting in September 1940. V1 was taken to Rechlin for further flight trials on 11 June 1940.

At this point it was decided that the BMW 139's overheating problems were beyond repair, and a new BMW design was allocated to the Fw 190 instead—the fan-cooled BMW 801 C. This incorporated elements of both the BMW 139 and an engine designed by Bramo, a rival firm that BMW had absorbed in 1939—the Bramo 329. Work on Fw 190 V3 and V4, which had fittings prepared for the 139, was halted. V3 was cannibalised for spares, and V4 was load tested to destruction.

The 801 C was roughly the same diameter as the BMW 139, slightly longer and 150kg heavier but promised to be even more powerful, more reliable and less prone to overheating than its predecessor.

Another change was the addition of the Kommandogerät device, which automated the adjustment of manifold pressure, compressor

ABOVE: Now fully painted, Fw 190 V1 is readied for yet another test flight.

gear shift, fuel mixture regulation, ignition control and constant speed control through propeller pitch.

The first prototype fitted with the BMW 801 C, Fw 190 V5, flew in April 1940. The extra weight of the engine meant that the Fw 190's airframe had to be strengthened to accept it and the undercarriage struts stiffened. In addition, the cockpit was moved further aft, and the overall length of the aircraft was increased by 68mm from 8.73m to 8.798m. As a result, the cockpit now remained cooler, and the extra space at the front of the aircraft allowed a pair of machine guns to be fitted onto its nose above the engine if required.

Earlier tests had revealed that above 270mph airflow over the aerodynamic cockpit canopy held it firmly in position, preventing the pilot from baling out. Designer Rudolf Blaser, who had been heavily involved in the Fw 159 and the original design of the Fw 190, therefore came up with a mechanism where a 20mm explosive cartridge pushed a piston that punched the canopy rearwards to the point where the airflow caught it and whipped it away.

Inspired by this innovation, test pilot Sander, who was also a qualified engineer, came up with a primitive ejection seat mechanism for the Fw 190, but he was unable to give the project his full attention, and when his initial efforts demonstrated that the explosive cartridges available were not powerful enough to propel the pilot far enough to avoid the aircraft's tail the idea was dropped.

The extra engine weight had a direct impact on the Fw 190's manoeuvrability—the wing loading had increased, and flight tests using V5 revealed the impact this had on the aircraft's handling. It was decided that the best way to overcome this was to extend the wings and while this was being discussed, prototype V6 was completed and took its first flight on 31 May 1940.

ABOVE: An unpainted Fw 190 V5 is wheeled across Focke-Wulf's Bremen facility. Shadowed in the background is an early Fw 189 Uhu. First flown in April 1940, V5 was the third Fw 190 prototype completed and the first to be fitted with the BMW 801 C.

Both V5 and V6 were each armed with a quartet of 7.9mm MG 17 machine guns—two in the wing roots and two on the nose. This configuration meant that they were retrospectively referred to as Fw 190 A-0/U1s. The 'U' stood for 'Umrüst bausatz' or 'conversion kit'—an 'Umbau' was a change to the aircraft's configuration carried out at the factory, or on rare occasions in the field by an accredited Focke-Wulf subcontractor.

After the two Fw 190 A-0/U1 aircraft, nine more A-0s were produced, taking their first flights between July and October 1940 and being used to test various weapons layouts, engine modifications and other experimental configurations.

Finally, on 10 October 1940, Fw 190 A-0 Werk-Nr. 0016 (the 16th Fw 190 built after the six prototypes and the nine A-0s), KB+PR, made its flying debut with an enlarged wing. Each wing tip had been extended by just over 500mm, giving it a wingspan of 10.5m, compared with 9.5m of the earlier examples. Wing area increased from 14.9m^2 to 18.3m^2, and the wing tips were given a squarer shape. Performance was still worse than the small-wing BMW 139 Fw 190s, however, with top speed at 5600m down from 695km/h to 686km/h and range down to 1080km from 1100km. Service ceiling was improved, though, from 11,000m to 11,400m.

The new wing was thereafter referred to as the V5g, and any Fw 190 without it was a V5k, the 'g' being for 'grosser' (larger) and the 'k' being for 'kleiner' (smaller), and was installed on all subsequent Fw 190 A aircraft.

In early 1941, Werk-Nr. 0007 became the prototype for the Fw 190 A-1 and was given the new production Werk-Nr. 190.0110.001. The 190 was the type, the 011 meant 'A-1', the 0 was the manufacturer—Focke-Wulf—and the final 001 was the individual aircraft's serial number. Other companies that later built the Fw 190 had their own numbers where

ABOVE: D-OPZE not only underwent a change of nose during its development, but also changed registration to the military code FO+LY. It made its first flight in this form on 25 January 1940.

ABOVE: A quartet of pre-production Fw 190 A-0s. The machine in the foreground, Werk-Nr. 0010, managed 30 flights with its BMW 801 C-0 engine—more than most of its contemporaries.

ABOVE: Test pilot Hans Sander fires up the engine of Fw 190 V1. The metal panel behind the BMW 139 engine's exhausts has already become heavily blackened.

Focke-Wulf had the 0. AGO had 2, Arado 5 and 6 and Fieseler 7.

As the template for the front-line fighters that were to follow, Werk-Nr. 190.0110.001 had a BMW 801 C-1 engine generating 1560hp at sea level, a pair of MG 17s over the engine and two more in the wing roots. There was also provision for the fitment of two 20mm cannons in outer wing positions.

The first Luftwaffe unit to convert to the Fw 190 was the II. Gruppe of Jagdgeschwader 26 (II./JG 26). In March 1941, JG 26 officers Oblt Otto Behrens and Lt Karl Borris were seconded to establish and lead an experimental unit, Erprobungsstaffel 190, at Rechlin-Roggenthin to ready the Fw 190 for active service. Both men had technical backgrounds and were given a team of 30 ground crew and half a dozen A-0s to work with.

Borris found the Fw 190 a pleasure to fly but realised that its BMW 801 C engine was the source of serious problems. He said:

> "Whatever could possibly go wrong with it did. We hardly dared to leave the immediate vicinity of the airfield with our six prototype machines.
> "Oil lines ruptured. The heavily armoured oil cooler ring in front of the engine often broke. The bottom cylinder of the rear row seized again and again, since the oil pump and the cooling surfaces were too small. Leaking fuel lines left the pilots in a dazed state from the fumes, unable to climb out of their aeroplanes unaided."

With Focke-Wulf's Bremen factory and headquarters now regularly being targeted by RAF bombers, plans were set in motion to construct a large new production facility nearly 600 miles further to the east—a 100-acre site at Marienburg, East Prussia, known today as Malbork in Poland.

ABOVE: This Fw 190 A-1, WNr. 0110.098, was used to test the Fw 190's ability to carry up to eight 50kg SC 50 bombs.

At the same time, much of the Luftwaffe's strength was being drawn to the east as preparations for the invasion of the Soviet Union, Operation Barbarossa, entered their final stages. By 28 June 1941, there were just two complete Jagdgeschwader (fighter wings) left in the west—JG 2 and 26—with a total of 140 serviceable Messerschmitt Bf 109 Es and Fs between them.

In July 1941, Behrens and Borris' unit was moved to Le Bourget airfield, near Paris, to begin the conversion training of II./JG 26. It was a slow process. Two of the new fighters were lost on 7 August when they suffered engine failure and crashed, and another on 9 August. Nevertheless, by the end of August the whole of II./JG 26 was working up on the Fw 190. The unit was then transferred to, first, Maldeghem and then Moorseele and Wevelghem, in Belgium. The first loss of a Fw 190 on the front line was to 'friendly' fire on 29 August, when anti-aircraft guns near Dunkirk opened up on 6./JG 26's Lieutenant Heinz Schenk. He was shot down and killed.

By October, III./JG 26 based at Coquelles, near Calais, had also begun converting to the Fw 190, and it was this unit's technical officer, Oblt Rolf Schroedter, who finally found a workable solution to the BMW engine's overheating problems. After the usual round of failures suffered by the engines of Fw 190s III./JG 26 had been given, Schroedter collected all the failed units and had them sent to his Gruppe's repair shop.

Examining all the failed engines together enabled Schroedter's team to determine that the exhaust system was to blame and that simply rerouting it reduced the temperature

ABOVE: During its early days in front line service it was not uncommon to see a Fw 190 dowsed in foam after an engine fire. It was only after several months with the Luftwaffe that a solution to the overheating problem was finally discovered and mostly cured with a re-routing of the exhaust system.

of the bottom cylinder of the rear row, thereby removing the single greatest source of engine failure on the Fw 190.

Schroedter's 'quick fix' was adopted as a factory modification, and soon BMW 801 C and later D units could run for more than 100 hours without heat damage.

From June 1941 to May 1942, Focke-Wulf built a total of 101 Fw 190 A-1 fighters. The next major upgrade, the Fw 190 A-2, had been prepared and subcontractors Arado, at Warnemünde, and AGO, at Oschersleben, were gearing up to produce it en masse.

More than this, the Fw 190 had now become a front-line fighting machine and was beginning to encounter enemy aircraft in the skies over France.

ABOVE: Fw 190 propeller fitting.

Chapter 3

Combat in the West

Although reports of a new German fighter with a radial engine had been received by the British in October 1940, it was not until January of the following year that these were confirmed as referring to a machine produced by Focke-Wulf, known as the Fw 190.

The weekly intelligence summary issued to all Royal Air Force (RAF) units, on 13 August 1941, included a report giving scant information about the Fw 190 but the very next day the two Spitfires of 306 (Polish) Squadron were shot down by two JG 26 pilots—Oberleutant Walter Schneider and Leutant Heinz Schenk—flying Fw 190 A-1s on their first operational sortie.

As well as being one of the first pilots to shoot down an enemy machine while flying the Fw 190, Schenk was also the first pilot to be killed in one. He was shot down by a German

ABOVE: The very first production Fw 190 A-1, coded SB+KA, was delivered to II./JG 26 and served until 18 April 1942, when it was crash-landed at Abbeville and suffered serious damage. JG 26 continued to make use of the A-1 well into 1942, although all had been written off, destroyed or rebuilt before the end of the year.

flak battery near Dunkirk on 29 August after his aircraft was misidentified as a target.

On 18 September a combat report by RAF 41 Squadron pilot Flying Officer Cyril Babbage stated that he had destroyed 'a Curtiss Hawk (or Fw 190)'. This was in fact the Fw 190 A-1 of II./JG 26's leader, Hauptmann Walter Adolph. Babbage, flying a Spitfire Vb, had been escorting three Bristol Blenheim bombers as they attacked a tanker off the Belgian coast.

Adolph and seven of his men, all piloting Fw 190s, had been assigned to protect the tanker. In the battle that ensued, two of the Blenheims were destroyed. None of Adolph's men saw what happened to him, and it was only when his body washed ashore at Knokke three weeks later that they knew he was dead. He was the first Fw 190 pilot to be killed in action.

Just three days later, a pilot of 315 (Polish) Squadron reported that he had shot down "one unknown enemy aircraft with a radial engine". This may have been Leutnant Ulrich Dzialas of 8./JG 26 who was killed that day or an aircraft of 4./JG 26 which crash-landed at St Omer after suffering engine failure following combat. By the end of September, II./JG 26 pilots flying Fw 190s had destroyed 18 Spitfires for only two confirmed losses.

On 13 October during another Blenheim escort mission, this time over the Fontinettes boat lift on the canal at Arques, near Calais, the gun camera of a 129 Squadron Spitfire took an image of what was clearly a Focke-Wulf Fw 190—rather than a Curtiss P-36 Hawk. JG 26 had 34 serviceable Fw 190 A-1 out of 55 in total by 25 October and a second Gruppe, III./JG 26, had started converting to the type. It already had 38 aircraft, but just seven of them were serviceable.

On 8 November 1941, the entire strength of JG 26 and Bf 109-equipped JG 2 was scrambled to intercept a double raid by the RAF. Two squadrons of bomb-carrying Hawker Hurricanes had been sent to target a distillery at St Pol, covered by five Spitfire squadrons, while a dozen Blenheims attacked the rail repair yard at Lille. The ensuing series of dogfights saw seven Spitfires destroyed for the loss of only three Fw 190s. Pilot Unteroffizier Karlheinz Kern of 4./JG 26 was killed, and two other Fw 190s had to make forced or crash landings, however.

On 22 December a single accident saw as many Fw 190s destroyed at a stroke as the RAF had managed all year. Oberleutnant Walter Schneider was leading 6.Staffel on a transfer flight from Wevelgem to Abbeville-Drucat at low level through heavy fog when he became disorientated.

He dived down over the Artois hills, instead of flying up over them, and crashed into the ground along with four of his pilots. All five were killed. Schneider was replaced by Oberleutnant Otto Behrens—who had previously led Erprobungsstaffel 190 in March 1941 as the Fw 190 was prepared for service.

In the wake of the attack on Pearl Harbor, Germany had declared war on the US on 11 December 1941, and the US had declared war on Germany in return. Up to this point, the only opponent facing the Fw 190 on the Western Front had been the RAF, and this would remain the case until the late summer of 1942, when the first American units joined the fight.

As 1942 began, however, poor weather meant that JG 26's fighters were involved only in occasional clashes with their British opponents. The Gruppenkommandeur (group commander) of III./JG 26, Josef 'Pips' Priller, scored one of the unit's few victories of the period when he shot down a Hurricane north-west of Calais on 3 January—his 59th victory.

The first major air operation of 1942 in the west was to cover a trio of German warships—the *Scharnhorst*, the *Gneisenau* and the *Prinz Eugen*—in what later became known as the Channel Dash. All three vessels had been docked at Brest harbour on the French coast for some months, the first two since 22 March 1941 and the *Prinz Eugen* since 1 June 1941. This put them within easy reach of British bomber bases, and nearly 3000 sorties had been flown against the immobile ships by February 1942. Hitler himself ordered that they be moved to German harbours, and it was decided to sail the trio up the English Channel, with the Luftwaffe promising full fighter cover for the operation.

The fleet set off at around 9pm on 11 February, and it was not until 11.30am on 12 February, after a pair of Spitfire pilots had sighted the fleet, that a British response was ordered.

Fw 190 and Bf 109 units were directed to meet oncoming RAF attackers at 12.16pm. Six Fairey Swordfish torpedo bombers of 825 Squadron took off to attack the warships at 12.25pm, but two of the three Spitfire squadrons ordered to protect them arrived too late. Only 72 Squadron made it on time.

As the Swordfishes and Spitfires approached the targets, they were met by Fw 190s of 8. And 9./JG 26 was led by JG 26 Geschwaderkommodore Major Gerhard Schöpfel. All the Swordfishes were downed along with three Spitfires, two Handley Page Hampdens and a Hawker Hurricane. The British, in return, destroyed three Fw 190s from 9./JG 26 and four other aircraft.

The *Scharnhorst*, *Gneisenau* and *Prinz Eugen* reached German ports on the evening of 12 February. All three had been damaged during the voyage, but the worst of it had been caused by mines.

Soon thereafter, JG 2 began to receive Fw 190 A-2s. The first of its squadrons to convert from the Bf 109 F was 6./JG 2, based at Beaumont-le-Roger. This proved to be a difficult process for the unit, however, and 11 Fw 190s were lost in accidents between February and May 1942.

On 17 April the RAF launched a daylight raid against the Maschinenfabrik Augsburg-Nürnberg (MAN) U-boat diesel engine plant at Augsburg. Twelve new Avro Lancasters, from 44 and 97 Squadrons, flew in two groups of six at treetop level across France to avoid German radar.

Diversionary raids had been mounted elsewhere to ensure that the Lancasters had a trouble-free trip, but the timing of the German response to these raids meant that Fw 190s of JG 2 were just coming in to land at Beaumont-le-Roger when their pilots spotted one of the Lancaster groups. Between 25 and 30 Fw 190s swiftly drew up their landing gear and gave chase. Four of the Lancs were shot down, only two made it to Augsburg and only one of these made it back to Britain.

By now, a few Fw 190 A-3s had begun to enter service too. Focke-Wulf built the first batch of three A-3s in November 1941 and had turned out 74 by the end of March 1942, while continuing to build Fw 190 A-2s using up existing stocks of BMW 801 C engines. Subcontractors Arado and AGO also continued building A-2s, but both started A-3 production in April 1942 and were joined in May by Fieseler.

Also that month, a third Jagdgeschwader, JG 1, began converting to the Fw 190. II./JG 1, based at Woensdrecht and Katwijk, in Holland, began receiving A-2s and A-3s on 12 May 1942.

As Fw 190 production increased, so too did complaints about build quality. These concerned irregularly sized wings made by contractors, poor wheel brakes, fuel pump failures, over-large control sticks, weak undercarriage bolts, leaky valves, poorly fitting cockpit canopies, too-short starter handles, woeful external paint finish and frequent engine failures.

Focke-Wulf remedied around a third of these with the Fw 190 A-4, production of which began in July 1942, and nearly all of them were addressed in the A-5, which entered production in November 1942.

Shot down by Spitfires 6 miles south of Dungeness on 26 July 1942, Leutnant Horst Benno Krüger of 5./JG 2 told the RAF intelligence officers who interrogated him that the engines of his unit's Fw 190s had had to be derated to keep them going for longer. He also said that the Fw 190s supplied to 5./JG 2 by Arado production were generally inferior to those produced by Focke-Wulf itself.

During the early summer of 1942, the RAF engaged in Circus operations: bomber and fighter attacks on targets inside occupied

ABOVE: Undercarriage failure was not uncommon among early production Fw 190s, particularly those manufactured by Focke-Wulf's subcontractors. KE+XQ, pictured here having suffered a collapsed undercarriage leg, was built by AGO.

ABOVE: The Fw 190 A-2 of Oberleutnant Egon Mayer, of 7./JG 2, some time between 23 June and 31 July 1942. Mayer scored his 53rd and 54th victories—both Spitfires—on 23 June. He was killed in action in 1944 with a tally of 102.

Europe intended to draw the Luftwaffe into combat in conditions unfavourable to them.

Instead, they tended to result in Spitfires getting shot down by Fw 190s. For example, Circus No. 178, on 1 June, saw a group of eight Hurri-Bombers being escorted to their target in Belgium by 168 Spitfires.

This large formation was picked up on German radar, and two Gruppen from JG 26 were scrambled to intercept them: I./JG 26, based at St Omer-Arques, and III./JG 26, at Wevelgem. When the Fw 190s caught up with the Spitfires off the coast near Ostende, they successfully 'bounced' them and shot down the wing commander plus eight of his pilots. Another five Spitfires were damaged in the melee. None of the Focke-Wulfs were damaged.

Against this stark backdrop, the Allies planned their first foray, in force, onto the German-held Continent. Both the Russians and the Americans were eager to see a second front opened up in the West and pushed for the invasion of France. What took place instead was Operation Jubilee, which involved attacking the strongly held port of Dieppe on 19 August 1942.

Canadian troops volunteered to take the lead, but little preparation work was done. A force of 6000 troops supported by tanks would land on the beach in front of the port and storm it. Aerial support came in the form of two squadrons of Hurri-Bombers, six of Hurricanes, four of reconnaissance Mustang Mk.1s, five of Boston and Blenheim bombers, three of the new Hawker Typhoon, 42 Spitfire

ABOVE: Fw 190 A-3 'Black 4' of 2./JG 2 stationed in France during 1942. Note the camouflaged hangar in the background with a Bf 109 parked outside.

ABOVE: A rare air-to-air photograph of an Fw 190 A-3 in flight over occupied France during 1942.

ABOVE: Fw 190s of 5./JG 2 at their base in France. During this stage of the war, Luftwaffe units could line up their aircraft without fear of attack. The D-Day landings changed all that.

V squadrons, two with Spitfire VIs and four with new Spitfire IXs. In addition, the Americans supplied recently arrived B-17s from the 97th Bomb Group for a diversionary raid. Opposing this aerial contingent were the Fw 190s of JG 2 and JG 26, the fighter units of both having now fully converted to the type.

On the ground, the Canadians were mowed down by overlapping fields of fire from bunkers, tanks sank into the pebbled beaches and the attack was abandoned. In the air, it was arguably the Focke-Wulf Fw 190's finest hour—JG 2 lost eight pilots, killed or missing, and six were wounded, but it claimed 67 enemy aircraft destroyed. JG 26 lost six pilots and claimed 38 victories.

The fighter-bomber squadrons of JG 2 and JG 26, 10.(Jabo)/JG 2 and 10.(Jabo)/JG 26, were also converting to the Fw 190 by the time of Dieppe, having previously operated Bf 109 F-4s. Their Fw 190 A-2s and A-3s were fitted with centreline racks to carry bombs, and operations began swiftly, with bombing raids on shipping around the Isle of Wight in early July. Throughout the remainder of the month and into August, the two Jabo units carried out nuisance hit-and-run raids. They also targeted factories along the south coast of England. The broad sweep of German attacks was narrowed down to targets in Kent and Sussex in October 1942—those closest to the unit's bases in France.

The British attempted to counter the Jabo threat by positioning five Typhoon squadrons on the south coast and lying in wait. This yielded some success and a pair of Typhoons from 486 Squadron bounced two Jabos from 10./JG 26 shortly after they had attacked

ABOVE: 'White 8' of 7./JG 2 was flown by Leutnant Jacob Augustin, who shot down six Supermarine Spitfires from 3 to 17June. He was killed on 15 July flying a different aircraft. 'White 8' missed out on attacking the RAF fighters flying cover for the Dieppe raid on 19 August 1942, having suffered damage four days earlier.

a church in Hastings, killing two civilians and injuring 16 others. One of the Fw 190s crashed into the sea, and its pilot, Feldwebel Karl Niesel, was killed. In his official report, the surviving pilot described that attack's target as 'a block of flats'.

Meanwhile, Hitler ordered that increased daylight raids should be carried out on Britain in retaliation for the RAF's night-bombing offensive. Canterbury was chosen as the target for a 'vengeance raid'; and the Jabos of JG 2 and JG 26 were joined by more Fw 190 fighter-bombers from III./ZG 2, and several dozen fighters from the other Staffeln of JG 2 and JG 26 were fitted with bomb racks, resulting in an attack force of 68 bomb-carrying fighters.

They were to be escorted to the target by 62 more Fw 190s while six carried out a diversionary raid. After waiting for the right weather conditions, they set out on the afternoon of 31 October and arrived over Canterbury at around 5pm, flying fast and low.

As soon as they were reported approaching the coast, barrage balloons were raised, and a number of the German pilots dropped their bombs off-target as a result. Nevertheless, 31 bombs hit the city and killed 32 people, as well as causing significant damage to buildings. Spitfires were scrambled, but, as before, the Fw 190s quickly turned around and sped back to France. Only a single Fw 190 from II./JG 2 was caught and shot down, its pilot being taken prisoner.

ABOVE: Focke-Wulf director Kurt Tank, right, is pictured with Josef 'Pips' Priller of JG 26 in September 1942. Priller was the highest scoring German ace on the Western Front at the time and shot down the highest number of Spitfires of any pilot during the war – 68. Despite being responsible for some of Germany's deadliest aircraft, Tank worked hard to maintain his civilian status throughout the war; hence his dapper outfit.

ABOVE: The last glimpse a B-17 crew might have of an Fw 190 before it either zipped up over their aircraft, fired directly into it or crashed into it head-on. This risky but initially successful style of attack was first used during November 1942.

ABOVE: The captured Fw 190 A-4/U8 of Feldwebel Otto Bechtold after he became disorientated and landed it at West Malling in Kent. Warning notices have been scratched into the matt black night-time camouflage paint. It is clear that the aircraft has no special adaptations for night flying.

ABOVE: A quartet of Fw 190 A-4s prepare for take-off from a temporary airfield in France during the summer of 1943. They are believed to belong to JG 26.

ABOVE: The Fw 190 A-4 'Black 12' flown by Hauptmann Bruno Stolle, leader of 8./JG 26, in France during 1943.

In addition to carrying out these raids, Fw 190 pilots were now also being called upon to intercept American Boeing B-17 daylight bombers. During the interception of a 32-bomber raid on 2 October 1942, the German fighter pilots encountered American fighter escorts for the first time—Spitfires from the US 4th Fighter Group and P-38 Lightnings from the 1st Fighter Group. During the ensuing skirmish, seven Fw 190s were shot down, compared with six Spitfires and a pair of P-38s. The odds were already evening, and one of the Fw 190s was shot down by a gunner on board a B-17—the first time this had happened. None of the bombers were shot down.

While the heavily armed Flying Fortresses lived up to their names, preventing the Germans from adopting the classic tactic of attacking from behind and below, the Luftwaffe sooner learned the best ways of approaching them. The leader of III./JG 2, Hauptmann Egon Mayer, came up with the strategy of a high-speed head-on attack—first tried, successfully, on 23 November 1942. Four B-17s were destroyed for the loss of just a single Fw 190.

The last glimpse a B-17 crew might have of an Fw 190 before it either zipped up over their aircraft, fired directly into it or crashed into it head-on. This risky but initially successful style of attack was first used during November 1942.

Although the successes of the Jabo raids had been relatively insignificant, the Germans resolved to intensify them as 1942 drew to a close. It was decided that a new sort of unit should be established to specialise in these attacks—the Schnellkampfgeschwader or 'fast bomber wing'. SKG 10 was to have three Gruppen, each comprising four Staffeln, compared with the more usual three.

Since existing Fw 190 pilots were all needed elsewhere, SKG 10 would be manned by former Bf 110 pilots drawn from the Zerstörer Gruppen or 'heavy fighter groups'. Meanwhile, the first Fw 190 unit had arrived in North Africa—III./ZG 2. Heavy losses inflicted by the British in the theatre had prompted Göring to promise that 40 of the new Focke-Wulf Fw 190 fighter-bombers would be transferred there to help.

III./ZG 2 arrived in Tunisia, having flown there via Italy and Sicily, in early to mid-November and flew its first mission against Bône harbour, held by the Allies, on 12 November. Five days later, II./JG 2 began to join III./ZG 2 at Sidi Ahmed. Its pilots were soon battling P-38 Lightnings of the 14th Fighter Group and B-17s of the Twelfth Air Force.

In December 1942, it was decided that III./ZG 2 would be renamed III./SKG 10 to become the third Gruppe of the new Geschwader, though it continued its bombing operations in North Africa—attacking Allied ground targets ranging from ships to tanks. In March of the following year, a third Fw 190-equipped unit moved to North Africa, II./Schl.G 2. In April, III./SKG 10 was issued with the Fw 190 A-5/U8, the predecessor of the Fw 190 G, but was deeply unimpressed with its vulnerable underwing 300-litre drop tanks.

However, it then began to receive the Fw 190 F predecessor, the A-5/U3s with added armour protection, and found that these were much better suited to the fighter-bomber role. Intense fighting followed, with hundreds of sorties being flown against advancing British forces but to no avail. All of the Luftwaffe's surviving Fw 190s in North Africa were evacuated on 8 May 1943.

During early 1943, the Jabos continued to attack the south of England, and during one raid on London on 20 January, a 500-kg bomb dropped by an Fw 190 landed on Sandhurst School, killing 38 children and six teachers. Elsewhere, the raid resulted in the deaths of 26 more civilians, with dozens injured. During training, it had been decided that SKG 10 should not only attack during daylight but during the night too. Therefore, on 16 April 1943, its pilots were ordered to attack England under cover of darkness.

The pilots had received very little training in night and instrument flying, and their aircraft had no special equipment fitted to enable successful navigation at night. It was a recipe for disaster. Two Fw 190 A-5s collided in darkness at Abbeville, killing one pilot, and another three collided on take-off at Poix, killing Oberleutnant Rudolf Trenn, the commander of 3./SKG 10. Yet another pilot was killed after being forced to bail out at low altitude over Kent, and three pilots became so disorientated that they tried to land at RAF airfields, thinking they were in France. Two crashed, but the third, Feldwebel Otto Bechtold, presented the British with their first fully functional captured Fw 190 fighter—A-4/U-8 W.Nr. 7155. It would later be given the RAF code PE822 and, following a lengthy evaluation, was eventually wrecked in a crash during October 1944.

ABOVE: Fw 190 A-3 belonging to JG 26 stationed at Wevelgem, Belgium in 1942.

Chapter 4

Fw 190 A, B and C

The development of the Focke-Wulf Fw 190 progressed rapidly as it was required to defeat the ever-improving fighters fielded by the British and the Americans. Many of the A-series Fw 190s were modified to better suit particular roles through the addition of factory-fitted or field modification kits, detailed in the appendix.

FW 190 A-0

The earliest serial production Fw 190s, the A-0s, were fitted with either the BMW 801 C-0 or the C-1. The first 11 had a 9.5m wingspan compared with the 10.5-m wings of the remaining 18. Although frequently fitted with different armament loads for experimental purposes, they were generally armed with six MG 17s—two on the nose, two in the wing roots and two in the outer wings.

The A-0s also had shorter spinners than later models, differently shaped armoured cowling rings and symmetrical teardrop-shaped bulges on the engine cowling to cover the interior air intakes for the engine. There were no cooling slots aft of the exhaust pipes on the sides of the aircraft either.

The first A-0 was ready in June 1940, and the last was completed in October 1941. A total of 29 were made—not counting the V1, V2, V5 and V6 prototypes.

FW 190 A-1

The BMW 801 C-1 was the standard on all A-1s. The outer wing MG 17s of the A-0 were replaced with 20-mm MG FF cannon. A new longer spinner was introduced, and the cowling bulges over the engine air intakes became asymmetrical—a feature that would remain for the rest of the A-series. The exhaust panels on either side of the aircraft remained unslotted, although some aircraft later had slots retrofitted.

The A-1 saw the introduction of the cartridge-fired cockpit canopy emergency opening system, and the pilot's head armour was a different shape from that of the A-0. The first batch of four A-1s were completed in June 1941, and production continued until November 1941. A total of 102 were made.

There were no cooling slots on the sides of the Fw 190 A-1's fuselage, aft of the engine exhausts, as seen on later models. 'TI+DQ' is an Fw 190 A-1/U1. It was shot down on 10 April 1942, over Abbeville, and the pilot, Lt Werner Michalski of 4./JG 26, was killed.

FW 190 A-2

The introduction of the new BMW 801 C-2 engine resulted in a new model number, the A-2. The engine featured a rerouted exhaust system that largely cured the overheating problems experienced by earlier versions.

Ventilation slots were fitted to the exhaust panels on the sides of the fuselage to further aid cooling. Armament was further upgraded from the A-1, with the wing root MG 17s being replaced with a 20-mm MG 151/20E cannon. The A-1's gunsight, the Revi C12/C was also upgraded to the C12/D.

The first A-2s were built by Arado at Warnemünde, rather than Focke-Wulf, in August 1941. Focke-Wulf's first examples followed

ABOVE: There were no cooling slots on the sides of the Fw 190 A-1's fuselage, aft of the engine exhausts, as seen on later models. 'TI+DQ' is an Fw 190 A-1/U1. It was shot down on 10 April 1942, over Abbeville, and the pilot, Lt Werner Michalski of 4./JG 26, was killed.

ABOVE: Cooling ventilation slots were first introduced on the Fw 190 A-2, an AGO-built example, 'KE+XV' being pictured here.

in September, and production by Focke-Wulf, Arado and AGO at Oschersleben (from October) continued until August 1942, with a total of 426 being produced.

FW 190 A-3

Another change of engine, this time to the BMW 801 D-2, resulted in another new model. The A-3 kept the A-2's armament and was similar to it in most other respects. The first A-3 was produced by Focke-Wulf in November 1941, and production continued in parallel with that of the A-2 for 10 months before the A-2 was finally dropped.

A-3s continued to be made until June 1943, with Focke-Wulf, Arado and AGO being joined by a third subcontractor, Fieseler at Kassel, from May to August 1942. A total of 509 A-3s were constructed.

FW 190 A-4

In June 1942, with production of both A-2s and A-3s still ongoing, the A-4 joined the production lines of Focke-Wulf and AGO. Fieseler and Arado also began producing it in July. Armament remained the same, but the FuG 16 Z radio set replaced previous models' FuG VIIa. This required a small radio mast to be fitted atop the tail fin and made it easy to distinguish an A-4 from its predecessors since none of them had it.

Some A-4s were also fitted with controllable cooling vents on the fuselage sides in place of the slots. Production of the A-4 ceased at Focke-Wulf in November 1942 and at Fieseler in February 1943. It was dropped from the Arado production line in June 1943, and AGO continued to produce it until August 1943. A total of 896 A-4s were made.

ABOVE: The Fw 190 A-3, though externally very similar to the Fw 190 A-2, was powered by the significantly upgraded BMW 801 D-2. Delivered to III./JG 1 during the summer of 1942, this Fw 190 A-3 continued in front-line use until it was finally destroyed on 3 April 1944, while serving with I./SG 101.

LEFT: Easily distinguished from its predecessors by the small radio mast on its tail, the Fw 190 A-4 was also produced in greater numbers. This example has the factory-fit U8 modification, making it a long- range fighter-bomber. The modification was later standardised as the Fw 190 G-1.

FW 190 A-5

The A-5 entered into production at Focke-Wulf's factories in November 1942, and Arado, AGO and Fieseler introduced it later. It was similar to the A-4 but had a 6¼in section inserted between the rearward edge of the engine cowling and the fuselage—moving the engine further away from the cockpit and improving the BMW 801's cooling. With this new longer nose, the A-5's length was 8.95m

ABOVE: 'GL+MY' was a standard Fw 190 A-5—a type produced in larger numbers than any other apart from the A-8. Its nose was more than 6in longer than those of its predecessors in order to further improve engine cooling.

ABOVE: An Fw 190 A-4 fitted with a pair of WGr 21 mortar tubes, one under each wing. This upgrade could be fitted in the field and was available for every subsequent type of Fw 190, except the A-9. Initially intended for use against heavy bomber formations, the WGr 21 launchers were also sometimes used against ground targets. The tubes had a significant negative effect on the aircraft's performance but could be jettisoned once expended.

compared with the A-4's 8.78m. The A-5 also had updated cockpit instrumentation and an Eka 16 gun camera.

Shifting the engine further forward also altered the aircraft's centre of gravity, enabling it to carry more weight further aft. Armament remained the same but a wide range of Umbau factory-fit modifications and Rüstsatz field conversion kits were produced for the A-5.

It was built alongside the F-2 and G-2 versions of the Fw 190, which has resulted in confusion over precisely how many were built. The combined total of all three was 1863 up to August 1943, when AGO finally stopped building them.

FW 190 A-6

The first A-6 was produced by AGO in April 1943, and the type was built exclusively by Focke-Wulf's subcontractors. The main difference from the A-5 was the replacement of the MG FF cannon in the outer wing positions with MG 151s. This meant armament was now two MG 17s on the aircraft's nose, two MG 151s in the wing roots and two more in the outer wings.

The bulker MG 151 required a bulge on the upper surface of the A-6's wing as well as the bulge that had already been required on the lower surface to accommodate the MG FF. In addition, the MG 151's longer barrel protruded further from the wing's leading edge—another visual identifier. The updated FuG 16 ZE radio navigation system was installed too, requiring a small 'teardrop' base and loop aerial to be fitted under the rear fuselage, with an extra 'whip'-shaped aerial behind it.

In addition to AGO, Arado and Fieseler, a fourth subcontractor built a few A-6s—20 being completed by Norddeutsche Dornier at Wismar. When production ceased in February 1944, 1137 had been built.

FW 190 A-7

For the A-7, introduced in November 1943, the two nose-mounted MG 17s were replaced with higher calibre 13-mm MG 131s. These were about the same length but weighed

ABOVE: Among the many Umbau modifications made to various A-5s, the U14 must be regarded as one of the oddest. The Fw 190 was ill-suited to work as a torpedo bomber, but, nevertheless, three prototypes were created. Note the jacked up tailwheel to provide sufficient ground clearance for the torpedo.

ABOVE: The primary reason for the existence of the A-6 was to accommodate a heavier cannon in the outer wing positions. It can therefore easily be told apart from previous models owing to the sheer length of the MG 151's barrels. This is actually the A-6 prototype, an A-5/U10.

ABOVE: Constant efforts were made to upgrade the Fw 190's already considerable firepower throughout its service career, and one of the heavier options for the A-6 was the R1 field-fit pack—two underwing pods, each containing two MG 151/20 cannon. This was the prototype for the design, an A-5/U12.

more. The A-7 also received an upgraded gunsight, with the Revi C/12d being replaced by the Revi 16b, and the tailwheel was enlarged from 350mm × 134mm to 380mm × 152mm.

The A-7 had the briefest production run of any Fw 190 A type—the last examples being built in March 1944, just five months after the first. It was manufactured by Focke-Wulf (150), AGO (270) and Fieseler (200), with Arado out of the picture, being still heavily engaged in building the A-6 up to February 1944. A total of 620 were made.

FW 190 A-8

The version of the Fw 190 built in the greatest numbers, the A-8 was planned in April 1943 and differed from the A-7 in having an additional 115-litre fuel tank fitted in the rear fuselage. This meant that the radio had to be relocated to just behind the pilot's seat. It was also upgraded from the FuG 16 Z to the FuG 16 ZY, which required an aerial mounted beneath the port wing centre section.

Mountings for the ETC 501 under-fuselage rack, which was an option on many previous models, had to be shifted 200-mm further forward owing to the new rear fuselage fuel tank. In addition, mountings for WGr 21 rocket tubes were fitted as standard. Later examples of the A-8 were fitted with a bulged cockpit canopy for improved visibility.

The A-8 was built in huge quantities at numerous dispersed sites. Focke-Wulf itself made at least 1579 from the first examples in March 1944 to the end of the war. Other companies involved were WFG, Heinkel, Weserflug, Fieseler, Arado, Concordia, LBB, AGO and Norddeutsche Dornier.

A total of around 5100 are believed to have been produced, but production figures are sketchy or entirely lacking for the period from December 1944 to April 1945.

FW 190 A-9

The Fw 190 H-1 (see Chapter 5) was redesignated A-9 in late March 1943 and was described in a report of April 15 as being the same as the Fw 190 A-8 but fitted with the BMW 801 F (later known as the BMW 801 TH). Since the introduction of the 801 D-2, BMW had been attempting to produce a version with improved power output without a significant increase in engine size. It finally achieved this in mid-1944 with the 801 S (later the 801 TS). It had the same capacity as the D-2 at 41.8 litres but produced 2000hp at 2700rpm at sea level, compared with just 1700hp in the same conditions for the D-2. To go with the BMW 801 S (TS) a more efficient radiator was fitted, along with a more heavily armoured oil tank. As a result, the cowling was lengthened by 30mm.

LEFT: Relatively few Fw 190 A-7s were made, this one being from 2./JG 1. The type had an enlarged tail wheel and heavier MG 131 machine guns on its nose.

ABOVE: The ubiquitous Fw 190 A-8—easily the most heavily produced Fw 190. The one pictured here flew with II./JG 26 from a temporary airfield at Boissy-le-Bois in the immediate aftermath of D-Day. It is being pushed under cover to protect it from roving fighter-bombers.

ABOVE: Another engine change, this time to the 2000hp BMW 801 S (TS), resulted in the Fw 190 A-9—the last of the A-series to see action. Note the bubble canopy and the broad paddle blades of the VDM-9 propeller.

The first production A-9, based on the Fw 190 V36 prototype, was built by Focke-Wulf at Cottbus in August 1944. Norddeutsche Dornier joined in during October, and Heinkel started to produce it during November. AGO and Arado also began to build the A-9 in January 1945. Details of exactly how many A-9s were built are scant, but estimates range from 500 to 1000.

FW 190 A-10

The Fw 190 Ra-7 received the series designation Fw 190 A-10 in late March 1943 at the same time as the Fw 190 H-1 became the A-9. The A-10 was to have been the same as the A-9 but with new tailplanes and no weaponry in its fuselage. By November 1943, however, the A-10's armament had changed to two MG 131s on the nose and two MG 151s in the inner wings. Upgrade options included two MG 151s in the outer wing positions, two MK 108s in the outer wing positions, two WGr 21 mortars under the wings or two MK 103s under the wings.

At this point it was planned that the wings themselves would be standard Fw 190 items but that the aircraft's undercarriage was to be shared with that of the Ta 152 H-2. The last known reference to the A-10 comes from a list of designs-in-progress produced by the RLM on 12 May 1944, when it is referred to, alongside the F-10, as a development of the A-9 and F-9, 'adapted to the needs of the front line'.

FW 190 B

The B-series was an attempt to create a high-altitude fighter version of the Fw 190 A. Focke-Wulf spent a year considering a huge range of potential alternative engines for its new fighter between March 1941 and March 1942—these included the BMW 801 E, F and J, BMW 802, BMW 803, DB 603, DB 609, DB 614, DB 623, DB 624, Jumo 213 and Jumo 222. The DB 603 and Jumo 213 appeared particularly promising.

In May 1942, it was decided that three new subtypes of the Fw 190 would be created—the B, C and D. The B would be an Fw 190 with a BMW 801 but configured for high-altitude operations, the C would have a DB 603 and the D would have a Jumo 213.

Work on the Fw 190 B began with the Fw 190 A-3/U7. The aircraft's BMW 801 D-2 had its Kommandogerät management system removed to allow finer manual control at high altitude, larger air intakes on either side of the engine cowling and adjustable cooling flaps. Armament was just two MG 151 cannon in the wing roots to save weight.

Three prototypes were built, and the first flew on 16 August 1942. Tests demonstrated only a small performance advantage over the standard A-3, in the order of 5-6mph at altitude. It had been planned to fit a turbosupercharger, but the only ones available at the time sat directly behind the engine and would have exhausted directly in front of the Fw 190's cockpit.

Between November 1942 and January 1943, two alternative high-altitude BMW 801 versions of the fighter were drawn up. The first had a large cylindrical turbocharger unit suspended directly beneath its BMW 801 in its own nacelle, with a four-bladed 3.4-m diameter propeller and 20.3m^2 area wings. It would have had a pressure cabin, was to weigh 4000kg, including 65kg of armour, and armament was to be two MG 151s. The second was an ultralightweight 3700-kg design with a BMW 801 D or E, 65kg of armour, 20.3m^2 area wings, no pressure cabin and a standard three-bladed 3.3-m diameter propeller. Neither of these designs were taken up.

Instead, it was decided to add longer wings to a standard A-3, plus a pressurised cabin and GM-1 nitrous injection for the engine. This was the Fw 190 B. Wingspan was enlarged from 10.5m to 12m 40cm on Fw 190 V12, but work on this was halted and a quartet of A-0s—W.Nrs. 0046-0049—were converted instead as Fw 190 B-0s.

The first Fw 190 B-0 was used to begin pressure cabin tests. Creating an effective pressure cabin proved more difficult than expected, however, and it wasn't until 9 January 1943 that a successful flight test took place with standard sized wing. More testing revealed that the cabin's glazing was ineffective at keeping the cold out, so a double-glazed version was developed that was heated using air from the engine. The aircraft was then fitted with the new lengthened wing, and tests continued into June. The standard wing was refitted in October.

Meanwhile, the second Fw 190 B-0 had begun flight testing in March with the new double-glazed canopy and a pair of MG 17s over the nose in addition to the two wing root MG 151s. While the guns caused no problems, the double glazed canopy was found to suffer from excessive condensation, limiting visibility.

The third B-0 first flew on 6 April with the double glazed canopy, MG FF cannon in the outer wings and a new heater designed to prevent the formation of ice on the cockpit. The fourth B-0 was used to test the installation of GM-1 equipment to boost engine power and had a 115-litre tank of nitrous oxide behind the pilot.

Before these tests were begun, back in January 1943, it was envisaged that a series of six Fw 190 B-1 production aircraft would be built, but this idea was dropped in the summer. Only a single Fw 190 B-1, W.Nr. 190 0210 811, was built and did not fly until 21 January 1944. It had a BMW 801 D with GM-1 injection, a pressure cabin, two MG 17s, two MG 151s and two MG FFs. A Fw 190 B-2 'normal fighter' version was planned with FuG 16 Z-E radio but no pressure cabin. None were built and the Fw 190 B series went no further.

FW 190 C

Development of the Daimler-Benz DB 603 was a protracted affair, and the first flight of the Fw 190 V13 test bed, W.Nr. 0036, did not take place until February 1942. A second aircraft, V15, W.Nr. 0037, had joined the programme by May. The V16 then followed.

Plans were drawn up to create two production versions of the DB 603 Fw 190—the C-1 and C-2. The former would have an unpressurised cockpit and an armament of two MG 131s on its nose and two MG 151s in the wing roots. The latter would get a pressurised cabin and an engine-mounted MG 151, MK 103 or MK 108 firing through the spinner.

In August 1942 it was proposed that the DB 603-powered Fw 190 should be fitted with an underslung Hirth TK 11 turbosupercharger. This was expected to result in an aircraft with 2000hp. It would also get larger wings and a pressurised cabin.

The modifications were made to Fw 190 V18, which was redesignated Fw 190 V18/U1. It first made two short flights on 20 December 1942, and test pilot Sander found that it tended to overheat, was tail-heavy and lacked power on take-off.

Other modifications to V18/U1 included an enlarged tailfin and a 3.5-m diameter VDM four-bladed propeller. Hirth experienced difficulties in developing its turbosuperchargers owing to a critical shortage of raw materials to produce sufficiently heat-resistant alloys.

An order for 727 Fw 190 Cs was placed by the RLM in December 1942 but this was cancelled on 26 January 1943, and Focke-Wulf was told to cease development of the DB 603-powered type. The company persisted with its testing of V18/U1, however, and by May 1943 it was able to achieve a respectable 416-mph at 36,100ft using its turbosupercharger. With this switched off, however, performance was diminished to 385mph at 31,150ft. Still, these results were enough to warrant another five being fitted with the Hirth TK 11.

The first of these was Fw 190 V29, which was fitted with a DB 603 S unit and sent to Hirth in June for use as a static turbosupercharger development airframe. V30 got a further development of the DB 603, the S-1, and first flew on 22 October 1943. Further test flights followed. V31, meanwhile, was written off almost immediately after it overturned on landing following its first flight.

V32 was completed in November 1943 and was also powered by a DB 603 S-1. It served as an armament test bed, being fitted with two MG 151s in the wing roots. V33 arrived too late, however, because by then all the remaining Hirth turbosupercharger test aircraft were being converted for use in another development programme that would result in Fock-Wulfe's Fw 190 successor—the Ta 152.

Focke-Wulf Fw 190 V1 D-OPZE. The first Fw 190 prototype, July 1939. *Chris Sandham-Bailey*

Focke-Wulf Fw 190 A-1 SB+KA, JG 26. The first production model Fw 190 A-1, 1941. *Chris Sandham-Bailey*

Focke-Wulf Fw 190 A-2 flown by Oberleutnant Egon Mayer, 7./JG 2, 1941-42. *Chris Sandham-Bailey*

Focke-Wulf Fw 190 A-3 flown by Oberleutnant Armin Faber, Stab III./JG 2, landed at RAF Pembray, 23 June 1942. *Chris Sandham-Bailey*

Focke-Wulf Fw 190 A-4/U8 flown by Feldwebel Otto Bechtold of 7./SKG 10, landed at RAF West Malling on 13 April 1943. 'Do Not Touch' was written in its night camouflage by its new owners. *Chris Sandham-Bailey*

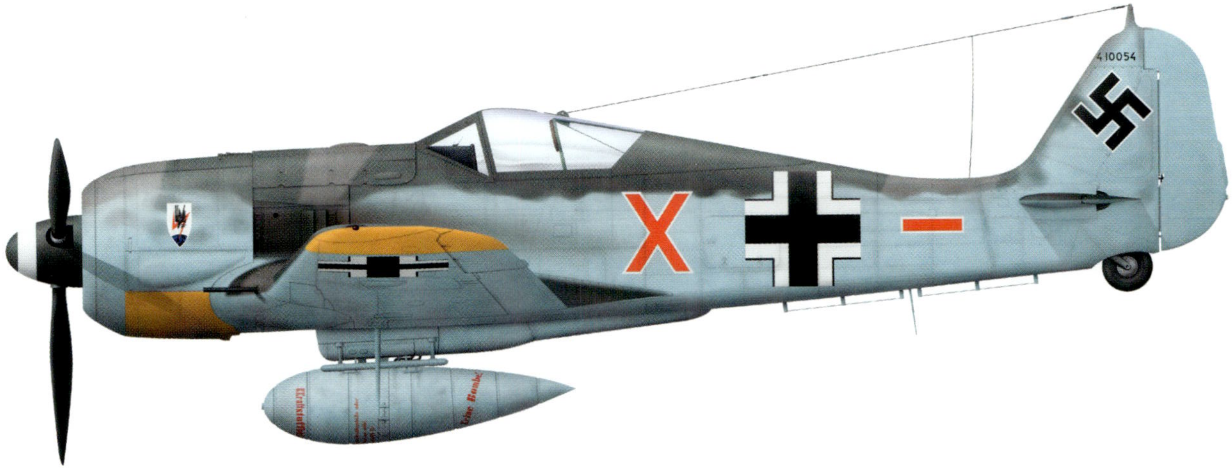

Focke-Wulf Fw 190 A-5 Werk-Nr. 410054 – the personal aircraft of Oberst Walter Grabmann, commander of 3. Jagddivision, 1944. *Chris Sandham-Bailey*

Focke-Wulf Fw 190 A-8/R2, Werk-Nr. 681382, flown by Hauptmann Wilhelm Moritz, IV.(Sturm)/JG 3, May 1944. *Chris Sandham-Bailey*

Focke-Wulf Fw 190 A-6/R11, 1./NJGr 10, equipped with FuG 217 Neptun, June 1944. *Chris Sandham-Bailey*

Focke-Wulf Fw 190 A-8, 5./JG 4, April 1945. *Chris Sandham-Bailey*

Focke-Wulf Fw 190 A-9, 7./JG 301, 1945. *Chris Sandham-Bailey*

Focke-Wulf Fw 190 F-3, I./SG 4, 1945. *Chris Sandham-Bailey*

Focke-Wulf Fw 190 F-8, 1./SG 4, northern Italy, spring/summer 1944. *Chris Sandham-Bailey*

Focke-Wulf Fw 190 F-8/R1, II./SG 2, 1944-45. *Chris Sandham-Bailey*

Chapter 5

Fw 190 E, F, G, H, S and Export Versions

Thanks to its adaptable airframe and inherent load-carrying capacity, the basic Fw 190 A ended up becoming a fighter-bomber and the de facto replacement for the Luftwaffe's ageing fleet of specialised tactical bombers.

FW 190 F

The first attempt to create a dedicated ground-attack Fw 190 was the A-3/U3, devised in May 1942. This had extra armour around and beneath its engine, on its fuselage sides and on the

ABOVE: The Fw 190A-5/U8, along with the A-4/U8, became the basis for Focke-Wulf's 'Jabo-Rei' long-range fighter-bomber. The aircraft pictured here is an A-5/U8 with the faired Ju 87 wing racks used for the Fw 190 G-1. Unusually, the drop tanks have been painted with camouflage.

undercarriage doors. Armament options proposed ranged from bombs to underwing cannon pods. Just 12 examples were constructed.

By the time the A-3/U3 configuration had been finalised, however, the A-3 series was over and the A-4 had taken its place on production lines. Therefore, an A-4/U3 option along the same lines was arranged. This time, however, the A-3/U3's centreline ETC 501 bomb rack was enhanced with the addition of the ER-4 adapter, which allowed the A-4/U3 to carry four SC50 bombs. Again, only a handful of these aircraft are believed to have been made.

Next came the A-5/U3 with two ETC 50 racks under each wing and a hefty total armour weight of 794lb. The A-5/U3 was scheduled for limited production in December 1942 with the goal of using it as the pattern aircraft for the full production Fw 190 F ground-attack aircraft, scheduled to enter into production in June 1943.

Focke-Wulf changed its mind in April 1943—at around the time that the Ju 87 was being officially declared obsolete—and the A-4/U3 became officially known as the Fw 190 F-1, while the remaining A-5/U3s became Fw 190 F-2s. A total of up to 270 are believed to have been produced.

The template for mass production Fw 190 F became, instead, the A-5/U17, which was built as the F-3. This was similar to the A-5/U3 but had its outer wing gun positions entirely deleted. Armament was a pair of MG 17s on the nose and MG 151s in the wing roots. It also had a FuG 16 ZS radio that used army frequencies, allowing the pilot to communicate effectively with the forces on the ground that he was supporting.

Most F-3s left the factory—they were all built by Arado—with a modification pack already fitted. The Fw 190 F-3/R1 had an ETC 501 bomb rack with ER 4 adapter under its fuselage plus two ETC 50s under each wing that could carry up to eight SC50 50kg bombs. These could be dropped all at once or in pairs using a control device fitted to the aircraft's cockpit known as the kleine Abwurfelektrik (small electrical release).

The extra weight of the bombs caused the aircraft to become extremely unwieldy and top speed dropped dramatically to just 326mph. Therefore, most had their nose-mounted machine guns removed during bombing missions.

Other modification packs were planned for the F-3, but few saw action. The F-3/R2 would have seen the aircraft fitted with a

ABOVE: Most of the Fw 190 F-3s produced left the factory in R1 configuration, which featured twin racks under each wing in addition to the centreline rack. This aircraft was also fitted with tropical filters—essential for flying on the Russian steppe.

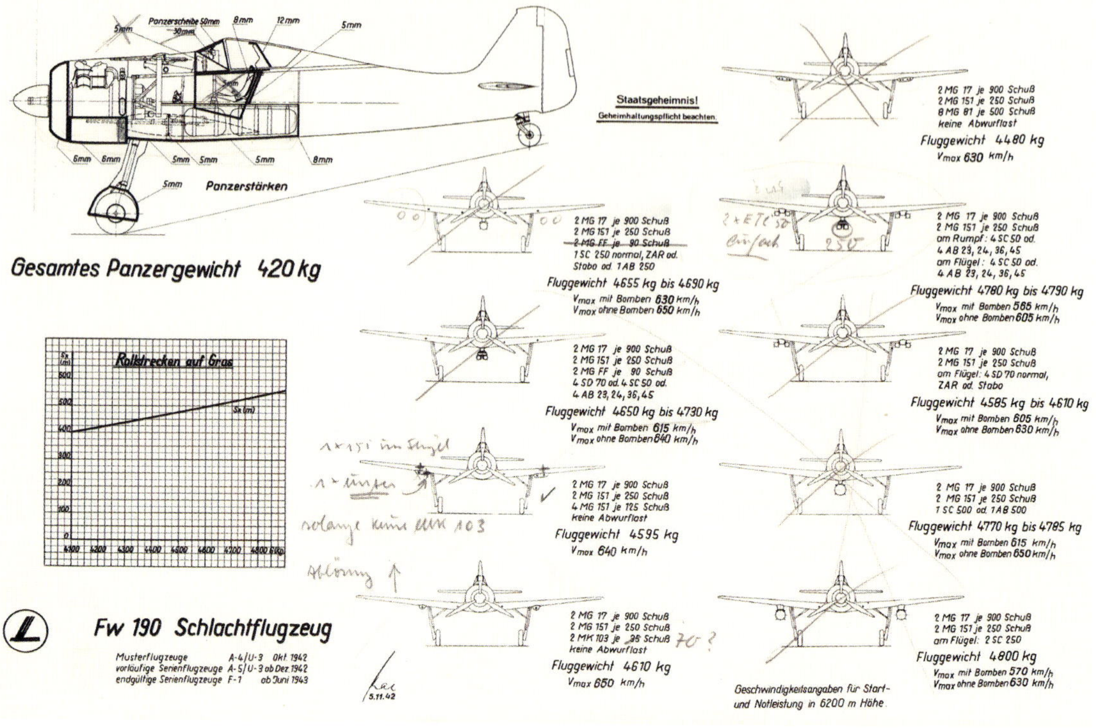

ABOVE: The planned development of the Fw 190 F-1 is made clear on this November 1942 Focke-Wulf type sheet—A-4/U3 October 1942, A-5/U3 December 1942, F-1 June 1943.

podded MK 103 cannon under each wing as a tankbuster, but in tests it was found that the MK 103's ammunition was incapable of piercing the Soviet T-34 tank's armour—making it unable to fulfil its primary function. F-3/U3, U5 and U14 involved the fitting of specialised racks to enable the aircraft to carry different types of air-launched torpedo.

Most of the 432 F-3s produced were built between April and December 1943. Production then dropped to a trickle until the last five were built during March 1944. The planned F-4 was essentially an F-3 with a released system that allowed bombs to be dropped one at a time, the F-5 was an F-4 with a BMW 801 F engine and the F-6 was an F-5 with a 'new planform' although what this would have entailed is unknown.

However, with the Fw 190 A-8 now in prospect and the A-5 airframe on which the F-4 was to be based becoming outdated, the F-4, F-5 and F-6 were cancelled, and a revised design was based on the A-8, to be known as the F-8. This had the same armament as the A-8 but without the outer wing positions. It also differed from the A-8 in having a modified injector on its compressor that gave enhanced performance during low-level flying.

A handful of conversions and upgrades had been made available for previous Fs, but the vast and unprecedented scale of F-8 production—almost on a par with A-8 production—meant the type had a wide range of kits added and modifications made. The F-8/U1 had a pair of ETC 503 bomb racks, one under each wing, enabling it to carry a pair of sizeable SC250 bombs, with the centre-mounted ETC 501 for a drop tank. This could also be used for a single SC500 bomb, but fitting one exceeded the Fw 190's maximum weight limit and dramatically reduced performance.

The F-8/U2 was intended to carry a pair of BT 400 torpedo-bombs on its wing racks,

ABOVE: The end of the line for the Friedrich—an F-9 captured by the Allies in Italy, in May 1945. Further extensions of the F series were planned but none reached full production, let alone front-line service.

and a specialised bomb aiming device, the TSA 2A, was installed in the cockpit. The aircraft's only other armament was to be the cowling-mounted MG 131 machine guns. Test conversions were made, but the U2 never entered full production.

The U3 was another torpedo carrying type, this time intended to carry a much larger weapon. It never entered into service either. Only one U4 was built, a night version of the F-8 with autopilot and improved electrical systems, and the U5 was similarly an upgrade of electrics only.

In addition to the Umbau conversions, there were seven Rüstsatz field modification kits—R1 was the form in which most F-8s were produced, with a pair of ETC 50 or 71 racks under each wing. R2 had 30-mm MK 108 cannon fitted in the outer wing positions, but only two aircraft were modified this way, by Dornier.

In contrast, up to 60 machines received the R3 modification—a 30-mm MK 103 cannon slung under each wing. It is possible that some R13s were made, a night ground-attack type with shields to mask engine exhausts from both the pilot and the enemy, and a few aircraft modified to R14, with a torpedo rack, entered into service with 11./ KG 200.

This last modification involved substantial changes to the F-8. The usual tail was replaced with the much larger item used on the Ta 152, the tailwheel was lengthened significantly to provide enough space for the underslung torpedo, and the BMW 801 TS engine was used in place of the 801 D-2. Armament was one MG 151 cannon in each wing root.

F-8/R15 was effectively the F-8/U3 renamed, and the R16 was developed from the U2, and only a handful entered into service. Overall, 3614 Fw 190 F-8s were built, 2264 of them by Arado and 1350 by Norddeutsche Dornier.

The A-9-based F-9, powered by the BMW 801 TS, had two cowling-mounted MG 131 machine guns and two MG 151s in the wing roots. It had the usual ETC 501 centreline rack, two ETC 50s under each wing and a FuG 16 ZS radio set. Production began in January 1945, and it is estimated that some 400 were built, though exact figures are unknown. There were five Rüstsatz—R1 switching the ETC 50 racks for ETC 71s and R13, R14, R15 and R16 matching those of the F-8.

ABOVE: When the ETC 501 centreline rack provided insufficient room for the required bomb payload, an ER4 adapter could be used. The photo shows the rack with a load of four SC50 bombs.

The Fw 190 F-10 was to have been the ground-attack version of the A-10, but this was never built. Focke-Wulf then jumped over the numbers 11-14 and began work, at the end of 1944, on the F-15. This was similar to the F-9 but had larger wheels. The main wheels were 740mm × 210mm (up from 700mm × 175mm), and the tail wheel was 380mm × 150mm (up from 350mm × 135mm).

The F-15 too was dropped before it ever reached production, in favour of an improved version of the design, the F-16. This was to be fitted with the BMW 801 TH, an improved radio set and the bigger wheels. The fuselage rack was the advanced ETC 504, and the wing racks were four ETC 71s or a pair of ETC 503s. Two prototypes were built, but the war ended before production could begin.

Finally, and perhaps incredibly, an F-17 was also planned. This was to have a TSA II D bombsight, the larger tail of the Ta 152 and a BMW 801 TS or TH engine. Full series production was optimistically scheduled for August 1945.

More than 4000 Fw 190 Fs were built, and the majority of them served with units operating on the Eastern Front.

FW 190 G

While the Fw 190 F was being developed, Focke-Wulf also worked on a long-range 'Jagdbomber grosser Reichweite' (literally fighter-bomber long range), Jabo-Rei for short. Based on the earlier A-4/U8, it had a centreline ETC 501 bomb rack and MG 151 cannon in the wing roots. The deletion of any nose-mounted weapons allowed for an additional oil tank to improve the BMW 801 D-2's endurance.

Focke-Wulf also bought in faired VTr. Ju 87 underwing racks from Weserflug, originally designed for the Ju 87, so that the Jabo-Rei could carry two drop tanks. Unfortunately, these racks reduced the aircraft's speed to an appalling 298mph. Two examples of the A-4/U8 were flown, the first on 19 October 1942 and the second on 8 January 1943, before the type was redesignated the Fw 190 G-1.

A Messerschmitt wing rack was then trialled, which consisted of metal stabiliser bars that fell with the tank when it was dropped—leaving only the wing-mounted release unit behind to cause drag.

A prototype based on the A-5/U8 was fitted out with these racks, and tests showed a dramatic reduction in the amount of speed lost. With the tanks dropped, the aircraft, W.Nr. 1488, was only 2mph slower than the standard A-5/U8. This design became the Fw 190 G-2.

A night version was also built as the Fw 190 G-2/N, based on the A-5/U2. It had screens on the sides of the fuselage to prevent the pilot from being blinded by flames from the engine's exhausts. It also had exhaust covers on the sides of the fuselage and underneath to prevent the exhaust flames from giving away the aircraft's position when flying in darkness.

With the G-2 in production, Focke-Wulf developed its own wing racks—which resulted in an 11-mph loss of speed when fitted. Nevertheless, the G-3 entered into production with Focke-Wulf fittings and was also built in a night version similar to the G-2/N. Conversions to G-3/U3, U5 and U14 were all devised to allow the G-3 to carry torpedoes. The G-3/R1 gave the aircraft the same armament as the A-6/R1—a pair of podded MG 151/20 cannon under each wing, four in total. The G-3/R5 reinstated nose-mounted MG 131s and added a pair of ETC 71 racks under each wing. All 550 G-3s were built by Focke-Wulf.

Plans for a G-4, G-5 and G-6, the latter two being BMW 801 F-engined, were dropped when it became clear that a major production drive would be made centred on the new A-8. The G-8 was to have the ETC 501 centreline rack plus an ETC 503 rack beneath each wing for the 300-litre drop tanks. The ETC 503 only caused a speed loss of 4mph. As with previous Gs, armament was reduced to the wing-root MG 151s, and the F-8's bulged canopy was also fitted. Focke-Wulf built all 146 G-8s as G-8/R5s in March and April 1944. These had a pair of ETC 50 or 71 racks under each wing.

Some Fw 190 Gs were field modified to carry very large payloads of 1000kg, 1600kg or even 1800kg. This was managed by

ABOVE: The first Gustav—a Fw 190 G-1 Jabo-Rei long-range fighter-bomber with 300-litre drop tanks fitted to its faired Weserflug racks, which had been designed for the Ju 87.

ABOVE: When Focke-Wulf finally finished its own underwing rack it was a masterpiece of engineering, but it wasn't quite as effective as the company had hoped and still resulted in an unwanted performance penalty for the aircraft to which it was fitted.

beefing up the landing gear oleo struts and fitting reinforced tyres.

Experiments were carried out to fit the Fw 190 G with water-methanol injection to boost performance, and a night-time version, the G-8/N, got as far as prototype tests, but when production of the G-8/R5 drew to a premature conclusion in April 1944, the G was wound up in favour of further Fw 190 F developments. G-9 and G-10 variants had been pencilled in, but these were scrapped.

Around 1300 Fw 190 Gs of all types had been built by the end of the war, though some of these were composites made using, for example, the undamaged wings from one wrecked aircraft and the undamaged fuselage of another.

FW 190 E, H AND S

Intended as a dedicated reconnaissance variant, the Fw 190 E never entered into series production. Instead, several Fw 190 A series types from the A-2 onwards were fitted out for reconnaissance duties, usually with the U4 Umbau modification. These had cameras, typically the Rb 50/30 or Rb 12.5/7 × 9, mounted in the centre of their fuselage pointing down.

During March 1943 the BMW 801 F-powered prototype Fw 190 V34 was given the series designation Fw 190 H-1. The engine installation differed from the BMW 801 D in requiring a new armoured oil cooler, a new radiator regulator and new oil pipework. The V35 and V36 were also allocated to H-1 testing, and in late March 1943 the H-1 was redesignated as the Fw 190 A-9. The 'H' was later reallocated to the Fw 190 Ra 8, which was eventually dropped in favour of the Ta 152 H.

In January 1944 the Luftwaffe High Command ordered the monthly delivery of training aircraft based on the Fw 190. These were to be the S-8, based on the A-8, and the S-5, based on the conversion of old A-2, A-3, A-4 and A-5 airframes. These aircraft had either BMW 801 D or 801 TU engines,

ABOVE: The G-3/N night version of the long-range Jabo-Rei fighter-bomber. Note the glare shield on the side of the cockpit to prevent the pilot from being blinded by his own exhausts.

no weapons, two seats in tandem and dual controls. Construction of the S-8 began in October to November 1944, while work on S-5s began between December 1944 and January 1945. At least 58 examples were made in total.

TURKISH FW 190S

The Fw 190 A-3 was offered to neutral Turkey in an export version known as the Fw 190 Aa-3, the little 'a' standing for 'auslandisch' (foreign). It had two MG17s on the nose and two in the wing roots, and an option of the MG FF in the outer wing positions. The FuG VIIa radio was fitted. Initially, it was manufactured exclusively by Arado, with five being turned out in August 1942, 10 in September and then one in October. Focke-Wulf and AGO then continued production. The Turks eventually received a total of 72 Fw 190 Aa-3s, which remained in service until 1949.

HUNGARIAN FW 190S

When Fw 190 A-8 production was dramatically increased at dispersed sites during 1944, there were aircraft to spare for Germany's allies. A batch of 16 Fw 190 F-8s were therefore given to Hungary in late 1944. These were accepted by the Hungarian Royal Air Force and were based at Börgönd, near Lake Balaton. In addition to the F-8s, which continued to be delivered in small batches after the first 16, the Hungarians also received a limited number of Fw 190 Gs.

JAPANESE FW 190

A single Fw 190 A-5 was shipped to Japan in 1943. It flew on a number of occasions before being taken apart so that its engine mountings could be examined as part of the programme to re-engine the Kawasaki Ki-61 'Hien'. The final fate of the Fw 190 A-5's component parts is unknown.

ABOVE: The double cockpit of the Fw 190 S-8 is evident in this photo, which also shows the dire shortages of fuel suffered by the Luftwaffe towards the end of the war.

ABOVE: Turkey's Fw 190s were fitted with a quartet of MG 17 machine guns with an option to fit MG FF cannon in the outer wing positions—an option that was exercised in this machine, No. 66.

ROMANIAN FW 190S

In August 1944, a coup was staged, which saw Romania forces turning their weapons on their former German allies. As part of this process, the Aeronautica Regal Romana captured 22 Fw 190 F-8s that had most probably formerly belonged to III./SG 10, based at Focsani-Süd. The aircraft received Romanian colours—yellow, blue and red—and nine were made ready for action.

ABOVE: The only Fw 190 ever to fly over Japan. The Japanese were generally not impressed with the type and made no effort to either produce it themselves or to buy further examples from Germany.

ABOVE: The Japanese painted their sole A-5 in their own colours, but no photograph has ever been found depicting its tail. How this may have been painted has therefore been the subject of much conjecture.

The day after Romania declared war on Germany, 26 August a Romanian Fw 190 was recorded as being shot down near Otopeni by Unteroffizier Schatermann of 3./ Transportgeschwader 5. This can probably be regarded as the only time an Fw 190 was shot down on purpose by the Luftwaffe.

When the Soviets entered Romania they confiscated the remaining Fw 190s.

YUGOSLAVIAN FW 190

A single Fw 190 F-8 of I./SG 2 was captured by Yugoslavian partisans towards the end of 1944. The following year the aircraft was put into service and continued to be used by the Yugoslavians until 1946. Parts of the aircraft, WNr. 930638, still exist at the Air Force Museum at Surcin, Belgrade, Serbia.

Chapter 6

Combat on the Eastern Front

Soviet forces were caught off guard at the beginning of Hitler's Operation Barbarossa and paid a heavy price for it. Luftwaffe Messerschmitt Bf 109 Fs were initially able to destroy large numbers of obsolete types such as the Polikarpov I-15, but by the summer of 1942 Soviet advanced fighters were appearing in huge numbers.

The heavily armoured Ilyushin Il-2 Sturmovik ground-attack aircraft was entering into service too, and the Western powers had sent hundreds of aircraft to bolster the Soviet effort, including Supermarine Spitfires, Hawker Hurricanes, Bell P-39 Airacobras and Curtiss P-40s.

The Eastern Front needed the new Fw 190 and the first unit to receive it was I./JG 51. During August 1942 it received one Fw 190 A-1, 10 A-2s and 32 A-3s before transferring to its new base at Ljuban, near Leningrad, by 6 September. Deliveries of the new Fw 190 A-4 began in October 1942, just as the first La-5s were reaching Soviet units.

II./JG 51 was withdrawn to East Prussia on 7 October so that it too could begin converting to the Fw 190, but with training still under way most of the Gruppe was suddenly transferred to the Mediterranean. Only 6./JG 51 remained behind to complete its conversion. 12 November saw III./JG 51 also being moved back to East Prussia to begin working up on the Fw 190.

By 22 November the German 6th Army was surrounded and cut off within the ruins of Stalingrad, and the Soviets were marching north with the intention of wiping out the Army Group Centre. German air forces in the area were I. and III./JG 51 with their new Fw 190s, plus IV./JG 51 and II./JG 3 with their original Messerschmitts.

The Luftwaffe's key objective was to prevent Soviet bombers and ground-attack aircraft from weakening the Army Group Centre still further—the Fw 190's first test on the Eastern Front.

The Russians deployed large formations of Sturmoviks on 4 December 1942, and both the Stabstaffel and I. Gruppe of JG 51 flew to intercept them. It was a resounding success, with 31 Il-2s destroyed. The joint highest scoring German pilots were the unit commander, Hauptmann Heinrich 'Gaudi' Krafft, Oberleutnant Edwin Thiel and Oberleutnant Heinz Lange, who each shot down five.

Just 10 days later, on 14 December, the Russians had their revenge on Krafft—his Fw 190 A-3 'Black <<' crash-landed near Kurkina after being hit by flak. It has been suggested that Krafft survived, only to be stripped naked, apart from his Knight's Cross, and beaten about the head by Soviet soldiers until he died. A unit of Panzer Grenadier Regiment 25 recovered his body from the crash scene but the source of the 'murdered' story has never been verified.

ABOVE: A pair of Fw 190 A-5s from I./JG 54 in flight over Russia bearing the Geschwader's familiar grüne Herz or 'green heart' insignia.

By January 1943 another Eastern Front Gruppe, I./JG 54, the Grünhertz or 'Green Hearts' had re-equipped with the Fw 190 A-4. It was just in time for the new Fw 190s to be used against Sturmoviks that were supporting an attempt to relieve the besieged Soviet forces in Leningrad.

It was now decided that the highly experienced Fw 190 pilots of JG 26 would begin transferring from France to the Eastern Front. I./JG 26 led by Major Johannes Seifert and 7./JG 26 were the first to go, being replaced in France by III./JG 54, which was still flying Bf 109s.

Arriving at Rielbitzi in northern Russia on 15 February 1943, JG 26 had been re-equipped with Fw 190 A-5s. It was now a part of Luftflotte 1, providing support and air cover for Army Group North. Its pilots soon found that battling the Russians was very different from fighting the RAF in the West.

The Russians tended to fly at lower altitudes, so most battles against them tended to be below 3000m. In addition, the much larger areas and distances involved meant that smaller formations of Fw 190s had to be used. The standard combat formation was a Schwarm of four or just a Rotte of two.

ABOVE: One of the best photographs in existence of Fw 190s in active service on the Eastern Front, this image shows a trio of A-5s from 5./JG 54 being readied for operations in northern Russia.

ABOVE: A Fw 190 A-4 of 2./JG 54 on final approach to a snowy airfield in Russia.

The certainty of safe haven in bases anywhere in temperate France, and the ability to bail out and be relatively sure of landing among friends, was replaced with the uncertainty of flying not only over hostile terrain but also over a constantly moving front line. It was often difficult for pilots, particularly those trying to land damaged machines, to work out whether they were likely to be picked up by friends or enemies.

One of I./JG 26's first tasks in this unwelcoming new environment was to operate in a fighter-bomber capacity against Russian ground forces attempting to crush the Demyansk salient—a pocket of German forces surrounded by the Red Army south of Leningrad.

The salient had been formed during early 1942 but had lingered on for almost a year, with the Russians now close to victory. JG 26 mounted attacks every day and, when the German army finally abandoned the salient, flew interception missions against Il-2s that were harrying the retreating German soldiers. From 18 February to 18 March 1943, I./JG 26 destroyed 75 Soviet aircraft, losing only three Fw 190s in return. Of the 75, 64 were claimed in a single day—7 March.

At the same time, JG 54 and 7./JG 26 had been embroiled in efforts to prevent the Soviets from lifting the siege of Leningrad, flying daily patrols in an attempt to close a relief corridor that had been established for the beleaguered city.

Further south, JG 51 was being stretched to help stave off a major new Russian offensive that was threatening to overwhelm Army Group Centre. On 23 February alone, the Gruppe destroyed 46 Russian aircraft. The next day it went one better by destroying another 47. Just one Fw 190 was lost, but more followed over the coming weeks as the Russians continued to press Army Group Centre hard.

IV./JG 51, led by Major Rudolf Resch, had withdrawn from the front line a month earlier to convert to the Fw 190, and by March all three Gruppen of JG 51 were flying the type.

On 15 April 1943, Hitler ordered the commencement of preparations for Operation Citadel—a pincer movement to be carried out by Army Group Centre and Army Group South to eliminate a Soviet salient around Kursk. Stalin's intelligence services managed to find out about Citadel well beforehand, however, by wringing it out of German prisoners under interrogation, and the Soviet air force was galvanised to prevent the blow from landing by carrying out a series of raids and assaults on the Luftwaffe. Large-scale bombing raids were carried out on German-held airfields between 6 and 8 May. Citadel was scheduled to

ABOVE: Luftwaffe operations on the Eastern Front were frequently hampered by appalling weather conditions. Here a couple of Fw 190 A-4s of I./JG 54 have been dug out of a snow drift at Krasnogvardeysk prior to a mission.

begin on 10 May, but such heavy damage was inflicted on German forces that it was decided that it should be postponed until July while reinforcements were gathered.

During May, a new semi-autonomous Fw 190-equipped fighter-bomber unit was formed in Finland, 14.(Jabo)/JG 5. Equipped with outdated A-2s and A-3s, its mission was to attack Soviet shipping along the Barents Sea coast and provide close support for German and allied forces in the Lake Ladoga area.

In addition, 4a Escuadrilla 'Azul' de Caza, a unit made up of Spanish volunteers that had spent some time in France undergoing training, returned to Russia in May equipped with Fw 190 A-2s. During June, I./JG 26 began returning to France, and JG 51 mounted a series of strikes on large formations of Il-2s while they were en route to bombing German airfields, causing heavy casualties for very few losses.

By early July, the force prepared for Operation Citadel was still inadequate, but time was running out, and it was therefore decided to press ahead anyway. Protecting the northern pincer as it swept down onto Kursk would be JG 51 and JG 54, both equipped

ABOVE: Another scene from JG 54's base at Krasnogvardeysk, where an Fw 190 has been covered with a sheet to prevent the guns over its engine cowling from icing up.

with a mixture of Fw 190 A-2s, A-3s, A-4s, A-5s and A-6s, plus some Bf 109s.

From the south, the Bf 109 Gs of JG 3 and JG 52, and the Fw 190 A-5s and F-3s of Schl.G 1, would provide the necessary air cover. The attack was due to begin at 3am on 5 July 1943, but as before captured German prisoners gave away the date and time under interrogation, and the Russians launched a massive artillery barrage on German positions just as Citadel was about to begin.

With the ground offensive stalled, the JG 51 and JG 54 set off on fighter sweeps at 3.25am with the intention of seeking out enemy aircraft and destroying them before they too could be brought into play on the front line. This proved to be a very effective operation, and by the end of the day, 360 Soviet aircraft of all types were claimed destroyed, 159 of which had been brought down by units using the Fw 190.

In return, German forces lost 98 aircraft. Just 12 of these were Fw 190s. The next day, 205 Soviet aircraft were claimed destroyed, 126 of which were by Fw 190s. On 7 July the third day of Citadel, the Fw 190 Gruppen downed 71 Soviet aircraft, and on the eighth day this total fell to 58.

Fw 190 victories over Soviet machines rose again to 66 on 9 July—a very high rate of attrition for the Russians—but they had now changed their tactics to avoiding a direct approach, preferring to take a wide route around the German front-line air defences and attack supply columns and airfields to the rear instead.

On the ground, Citadel had stalled by 10 July. The Russians had prepared extensive fortifications around Kursk, and the German tank armies were running out of fuel. The Luftwaffe too was experiencing shortages, allowing Il-2s to strike at German front-line units unopposed on some occasions.

German armour losses had reached 50% by the end of 12 July, and the Fw 190s of JG 51 and JG 54 were engaged in bitter battles overhead against MiG-3s, Yak-1s and La-5s as more Il-2s slipped through and destroyed German supplies to the rear.

ABOVE: This Fw 190 A-4 of I./JG 54 wears mottled winter camouflage.

ABOVE: A Fw 190 A-4 of I./JG51 at Dvoevka Vyazma about 200km west of Moscow.

Still, the Luftwaffe poured in reinforcements and on 13 July Fw 190s claimed 174 enemy aircraft destroyed. That night, German forces began a retreat at several points along the front.

By 15 July JG 51 alone had lost 63 Fw 190s. Hitler cancelled Citadel on 16 July, but there was no let-up for the Luftwaffe as the attack became a retreat, with the victorious Russians pursuing the battered German survivors westwards.

A fortnight after the start of Citadel, IV./JG 51 had lost a full third of its pilots and every single one of its Fw 190s, being re-equipped with Bf 109 G-4s and G-6s instead since these were more readily available. By the end of July, the Luftwaffe's Fw 190 strength in the east had been more than halved. JG 51 and JG 54 had claimed 1250 victories for the month, which even accounting for inaccuracies was substantial—but it wasn't enough.

The Soviet air force was easily able to make good these losses and now outnumbered the Luftwaffe in fighter strength by more than four to one.

Having been severely mauled by the ever-growing Soviet tank armies, the Germans were forced to begin a general withdrawal during late August 1943. The Luftwaffe too had suffered losses of men and machines that it was struggling to replace.

There were now simply too many Soviet tanks in the field for I./Schl.G 1's Fw 190 fighter-bombers to cope with. The unit was exhausted from flying constant sorties, and by early September it was being used to try and stem the tide of Soviet tanks that were breaking through around the Ukrainian capital Kiev. The leader of 1./Schl.G 1, Hauptmann Johannes Meinecke was shot down and killed by flak near Mutino on 4 September. II./Schl.G 1 was carrying out similar operations from Stalino, now known as Donetsk, in Ukraine but it too found that it just didn't have enough aircraft to make any impression. Stalino fell in early September.

There was a lull in the offensive against Kiev during October, but on 3 November 1943, the Soviets launched an all-out surprise assault on the Ukrainian capital. The defenders were overwhelmed by the sheer weight of numbers. The fighting around Kiev went on until late December when extremely cold weather brought a brief respite from further offensive action.

ABOVE: An unusual survivor, this early Fw 190 A-3 is pictured in 1944, serving with 1./JG 5 at Immola airfield in Imatra, southern Finland.

It had been intended that every Junkers Ju 87 on the Eastern Front would be replaced with a Fw 190 by the end of 1943, but there was a critical shortage of Fw 190s owing to the regular American and British bombing raids on production facilities. Those aircraft that were manufactured went straight to those units charged with protecting the Reich from the bombers. As a result, the ponderous and vulnerable Stuka continued in front-line service.

From north to south, the units equipped with the Fw 190 on the Eastern Front at the beginning of 1944 were 14.(Jabo)/JG 5 on the Finnish front, which had by then flown more than 1000 sorties and sunk 39,000 tons of shipping; 4./JG 54 with Luftflotte 1 in north Russia, which only had 10 Fw 190s remaining; with Army Group Centre with Luftflotte 6 were the Stab, Stabstaffel, I. and III./JG 51 and the Stab of I./JG 54 plus the Spanish Staffel 15./JG 51.

With Luftflotte 4 on the southern portion of the front was II./JG 54, though not its 4. Staffel, plus four recently established Schlachtgruppen, II./SG 2, I. and II./SG 10 and II./SG 77. While most of these units had a mixture of Fw 190 A-4s, A-5s and A-6s, the latter had Fw 190 F-2s, F-3s and G-3s.

Bad weather along the front meant very little flying was possible until 10 January. There were a handful of skirmishes with Il-2s, LaGG-3s and Airacobras, but it was the ground-attack SG units that were the most active, with II./SG 2 flying 42 sorties against Soviet vehicles and infantry positions on 12 January.

The first significant offensive of the year began on 14 January, when the Soviet 2nd Assault Army tried yet again to raise the siege

ABOVE: From one extreme to another. With the winter snows a distant memory, the personnel of 4./JG 54 sweat in the heat as they work on a Fw 190 A-6 in July 1944. Fourteen Ju 87s fly overhead—the type still in service long after it had been earmarked for replacement by the Fw 190.

ABOVE: A pair of Fw 190 F-8s from II./SG 77 on the Eastern Front in 1944. The aircraft closest to the camera shows clear spaces under its wings where the bomb racks have been removed. By this stage of the war, the Schlachtgruppen were frequently called upon to fly fighter intercept missions against Soviet bombers.

of Leningrad—which had been in continuous effect for around 900 days by this point. Freezing temperatures and poor visibility kept Fw 190s in the sector grounded initially, but the following day 6./JG 54 was able to tackle a flight of Petlyakov Pe-2 dive bombers and their La-5 escorts en route to attack German ground forces.

ABOVE: Final preparations are made to a Fw 190 of II./SG 2 prior to a mission in the spring of 1944.

On 24 January, the Russians launched a surprise offensive in Ukraine. Four days later, large armoured formations had successfully encircled 56,000 German soldiers and their vehicles at Cherkassy—forming the 'Korsun-Cherkassy pocket'. II./JG 54 was called upon to prevent Soviet aircraft from shooting down the Junkers Ju 52 transports being used to airlift supplies to the encircled armies. On 30 January the Soviets overran Siverskaya, which had served as JG 54's base of operations for several months.

By 5 February the Russians had advanced 200 miles westwards, but a German counter-attack was mounted, which then became a counter encirclement on direct orders from Hitler.

III Panzer Corps attacked northwards towards the pocket, but its advance was halted by fuel shortages on the evening of 16 February. This solidified into a Soviet counter-attack by the 5th Guards Tank Army, forcing III Panzer Corps onto the defensive—but it was still four miles from the pocket. The besieged force in the Korsun-Cherkassy pocket was told that it was now or never: it had to break out, starting at 11pm.

That night, huge formations of Il-2s hit the pocket with incendiaries, and the Luftwaffe was unable to challenge them. Rockets and artillery fire also poured in. Leaving behind 1450 wounded men who were unable to walk, the surviving Germans formed three assault columns and marched into the night with bayonets fixed.

Within 30 minutes, several battalions and regiments had broken through, reaching III Panzer Corps by 4.10am. The leader of forces in the pocket, General Wilhelm Stemmermann, remained behind with a rearguard of 6500 men.

When the Soviets realised what was happening, they reacted by employing overwhelming force. The 20th Tank Corps brought in a brigade of new Joseph Stalin 2 heavy tanks. These, along with dozens of T-34s, rolled into the columns of unprotected German support, headquarters and medical units who had been following the initial wave of assault troops through the breakout corridor.

It was a massacre that proceeded without challenge from the Luftwaffe. At the end of February, the shortage of Fw 190s was so critical it was decided that JG 51 should actually convert to the Bf 109 G-6, which was still in plentiful supply. This began in April and had mostly been completed by May.

The only Fw 190s now remaining on the Eastern Front were those employed by JG 54 and the Schlachtgruppen, of which there were now five with the redesignation of 14.(Jabo)/JG 5 as 4./SG 5. The latter were increasingly called upon to act as fighters against Soviet bombers, rather than ground-attack aircraft, as the German front line began to disintegrate under fresh offensives in March 1944.

There was some respite for German ground forces in April when the spring thaws turned previously passable roads into muddy quagmires, but there was no let-up in the air, with JG 54 flying sorties around the clock. The SGs were also hard-pressed. By the end

ABOVE: Heavily weathered Fw 190s of an unidentified Schlachtgruppe on the Eastern Front.

of April, II./SG 2 had only three or four serviceable Fw 190s.

Help was coming, however. The newly formed III./SG 10 had just become operational in Poland, with its first batch of Fw 190 F-8s, and on 15 May III./SG 3 was sent to Czechoslovakia to begin conversion to the Fw 190 F-8. It was transferred to the Eastern Front, on the Russian-Latvian border, on 27 June.

The arrival of the F-8 was thanks to a reorganisation of the German aircraft industry that negated the effects of the constant Allied bombing by dispersing manufacturing facilities far and wide across Germany. Hundreds more Fw 190s were now pouring off production lines, ending the crippling shortages seen on the Eastern Front and setting the stage for the final year of the war.

Chapter 7

Last Defence of the Reich

During the spring of 1943, as both American daylight bombing and British night bombing intensified, the Luftwaffe came under increasing pressure to prevent it.

While tactics had been developed that enabled the Fw 190 to tackle American B-17s and B-24s, particularly with WGr 21 mortars, the Royal Air Force's (RAF's) bombers were more difficult to stop. When combined into a single stream, it was impossible for German controllers on the ground to direct night fighters onto individual targets.

In addition, from April 1943, the British were able to jam the German Lichtenstein B/C radar and then the C-1 that followed it. While the 'battle of the beams' went on, with both sides trying to improve their radars and radar jamming technology, German night fighter production failed to keep pace with the sheer number of bombers that the RAF was able to field night after night.

Luftwaffe pilot Oberstleutant Hans-Joachim Herrmann came up with a solution—he thought that single-seat fighters, working closely with searchlights and flak, could be sent up at night to tackle enemy bombers by sight alone. These operations were dubbed Wilde Sau or 'wild boar'. An improvised unit was set up, Nachtjagdversuchskommando Hermann, on 20-22 April 1943, and training of pilots began. The first major Wilde Sau operation, using Fw 190s, took place on 3 July 1943 over Köln.

It was a disaster—the flak and searchlights ignored instructions, lighting up both the bombers and Hermann's fighters indiscriminately, while the flak seemed to fire at random. Nevertheless, the Wilde Sau crews did shoot down six British bombers. Now Hermann was given a mixed force of eight unmodified Fw 190s, including A-4s, A-5s and A-6s, plus 33 Bf 109 G-6s and a single Bf 109 T. The unit was initially dubbed 'JG Hermann' but renamed JG 300 on 20 August 1943. Operations continued from the end of July up to 26 September, when two additional units were formed—JG 301 and JG 302. Only II./JG 301 flew the Fw 190, though, and it shared its aircraft with I./JG 11, which used them during the day.

Flying a single-seat fighter at night without radar and with radio frequencies often heavily jammed was extremely dangerous, and losses were high. Pilots were trained to bail out if they became confused, ran out of fuel or suffered damage, rather than risk a crash in darkness.

Kurt Tank was reportedly impressed by this previously unforeseen use for his fighter and set about developing a version of the Fw 190 A-6 equipped with a FuG Neptun airborne intercept radar. Successful experiments were conducted with the FuG 216 Neptun V, the aircraft fitted with it being able to independently detect enemy bombers.

Several of these experimental airframes were used in combat by 2./JG 2 to shoot down a number of Halifax bombers in November 1943. In December an Fw 190 A-5, WNr. 181703 CI+PU was fitted with the FuG Neptun 216 R tail warning radar.

'BIG WEEK' AND BERLIN

A new air fleet, Luftflotte Reich, was formed on 1 January 1944, and it included Fw 190-equipped units JG 1, JG 11, JG 300 and JG 302. Four days later JG 1 and JG 11 were in action against American bomber formations and their fighter escorts.

Further raids took place on 7 and 11 January, but by far the largest was on 29 January, when more than 800 bombers and 630 fighters targeted Frankfurt. Fw 190-flying I./JG 26 and II./JG 26 intercepted them over France both on the way there and on the way back, claiming just 11 B-17s, five B-24s and five fighters destroyed. Three Fw 190 pilots were killed.

Another raid the following day had a similar outcome for the Allies, but this time with 11 German pilots killed. Frankfurt was hit again on 4 February and again on 8 February. Further raids followed, and on 19 February the Americans launched 'Big Week' or Operation Argument. This involved 1000 bombers and hundreds of fighters—every operational fighter available to the Eighth and Ninth Air Forces.

The goal was to cripple the German aircraft manufacturers, and targets included the works of Arado, Heinkel, Erla, Junkers and AGO. I./JG 11, I. and II./JG 1 and II./JG 26 all attempted interceptions with their Fw 190s but destroyed only 21 bombers and four fighters.

The following day, more than 860 bombers hit factories and Luftwaffe airfields.

ABOVE: A Focke-Wulf Fw 190 lies broken and upside down amid the wreckage around the Reichstag building in Berlin. The fighter was flown by several units during the last defence of the city.

The pounding continued until 25 February, concluding with an attack on Messerschmitt's factories at Augsburg and Regensburg with a force of 754 bombers and 899 fighters.

'Big Week' did not have the overall impact that the Allies had hoped it would, and by late March 1944 most of the damage had been repaired. However, around 240 Luftwaffe pilots had been killed and 140 more wounded. The majority of four-engined bombers shot down had been dispatched by Bf 109s.

On 6 March the Americans bombed Berlin with 730 B-17s and B-24s, killing 345 civilians. The Americans, however, paid a high price for this attack, with 69 bombers shot down, a staggering 347 damaged and 11 fighters destroyed. One of the B-17s had even been rammed by a Fw 190 of Sturmstaffel 1.

The Luftwaffe thought this might cause the Americans to pause their attacks, but two days later there was another raid on Berlin, this time with a depleted force of 470 bombers. On 18 March there was a large-scale bombing raid on airfields in the Munich area, and I./JG 11 managed to destroy 10 B-24s without losing a single Fw 190. Berlin was attacked again on 23 March, this time by 768 bombers.

The Fw 190 units continued to score victories, but it was never enough. This pattern continued throughout April and May before the Americans switched their attention again, this time to German oil production. The end of May saw Allied bombers hitting targets up and down the French coast in preparation for Operation Overlord—the D-Day invasion.

D-DAY

With the carnage going on over Germany and on the Eastern Front, the Luftwaffe in France had been thoroughly drained of its strength by 6 June 1944. JG 2 and JG 26 had just 92 serviceable fighters when the Allies began their landings at Normandy—79 Fw 190s and 13 Bf 109s.

ABOVE: Josef 'Pips' Priller poses with his BMW 335 in front of one of his many Fw 190 'Black 13' aircraft in 1943. A year later, his was one of the few Luftwaffe aircraft to attack the invasion beaches on D-Day—6 June 1944.

Ground-attack, fighter-bomber and night fighter Fw 190s amounted to another 37. The first Fw 190 victory of D-Day came when Hauptmann Helmut Eberspächer of 3./SKG 10 shot down four Avro Lancasters of 97 Squadron just after 5am.

Four hours later, Oberstleutnant Josef Priller and Unteroffizier Heinz Wodarczyk of Stab/JG 26 flew over Sword Beach in Fw 190 A-8s. On seeing the hundreds of vessels arrayed before him, Priller reportedly said: "What a show! What a show!" The pair famously made a single strafing pass before fleeing into the clouds as dozens of anti-aircraft guns opened fire on them.

Half an hour later, I./JG 2 Fw 190 A-8/R6s attacked landing craft at low level with WGr. 21 mortars. Starting the day with around 14 serviceable aircraft, I./JG 2 ended it with just three. Units from Germany began moving to France to cover ground forces attempting to contain the landings, but these suffered too, with III./SG 4 losing four aircraft while moving to Laval.

Fw 190 units moved up to oppose the Allies included elements of JG 1, JG 3, JG 11 and JG 54. Attempts to actually fight the British and Americans were hampered by continual raids on their airfields. A few days later, 7./JG 51 also moved to France from Russia, having been re-equipped with Fw 190 A-8s.

Leutnant Günther Heckmann of 7./JG 51 described the situation his unit found on arrival thus:

> "We quickly learned the rules for survival in Normandy. Mustangs and Thunderbolts continually circled and dived as soon as they saw their prey. The only possibility of escaping them was to bank and engage them in a turning dogfight.

"Nerves of steel were required. Pilots who tried to flee had no chance—the Americans would catch them in seconds. Typhoons, Tempests and Spitfires were the aircraft which were capable of dogfighting."

It was chaos, and although the Germans managed their share of successes, for example when Hauptmann Emil 'Bully' Lang of II./JG 26 shot down four P-51 Mustangs in four minutes on 20 June and destroyed another four on 24 June, it was clear that they were struggling to combat the roving Allied fighters effectively.

After the Americans achieved a breakthrough with Operation Cobra on 27 July, German forces began a retreat from western France, and the exhausted fighter units were removed from the front line, one at a time, for rest and re-equipment at bases in Germany. Another two Fw 190 Gruppen were formed at the end of the month when heavy fighter units I. and II. ZG 26 were redesignated I. and II./JG 6 and began conversion to the Fw 190 A-8.

It took longer than expected to bring the various Fw 190 units back up to strength, however, and JG 6 was not ready for action until 22 August, when II./JG 6 was finally transferred to its new base at Reims in eastern France. During its first operation, on 25 August, its 40 Fw 190s ran into a large formation of P-38 Lightnings from the 367th Fighter Group. In the ensuing melee 16 Fw 190s were destroyed compared with 11 P-38s.

By this time, SKG 10's fighter-bomber Fw 190s had flown almost 3000 sorties over the invasion area and then across France as the Allies began to rapidly advance. Both its pilots and its stock of aircraft had been severely depleted. III./SG 4 had been almost wiped out.

When the Operation Market Garden landings took place in Holland on 17 September 1944, the two closest Fw 190 units, I. and II./JG 26 tried to intercept the waves of transports and gliders as they made for the drop zone but were headed off by Spitfires and Mustangs. Further clashes during the course of the operation saw the German fighter forces again coming off worst. On the last day of the action, 27 September 1944, I. and

II./JG 26 shot down five Spitfires, but lost six Fw 190s.

During late September and early October, the first Fw 190 A-9s and D-9s were introduced, and the Wilde Sau night fighter Gruppen of JG 301 began converting from the Bf 109 to Fw 190 A-8s, which by now were being churned out in prodigious quantities.

One of the first tasks of the D-9-equipped 9./JG 54 and 12./JG 54 was to watch over the Messerschmitt Me 262s of Kommando Nowotny as they were taking off and landing at Achmer and Hesepe. The jets were extremely vulnerable during these stages of flight owing to their poor acceleration.

OPERATION BAGRATION

The Russians launched their largest offensive to date on the Eastern Front, Operation Bagration, on 22 June 1944, and the Germans were caught off guard. The Soviet Air Force put up hundreds of aircraft, and the depleted Luftwaffe, with units having been transferred to the West to fight the Allies in Normandy, struggled to fight back. Luftflotte 6 had 173 Fw 190s—but just 17 of these were dedicated fighters, the remainder being fighter-bombers. These suffered heavy losses as they were called upon to act as fighters in an effort to prevent wave after wave of Il-2s from destroying German ground forces.

By the second week of July, the Army Group Centre was disintegrating, and another major assault was under way in Ukraine that the Luftwaffe was again ill-equipped to deal with, resulting in significant losses to the Fw 190s of II./SG 2, II./SG 10, SG 77 and 1./NAGr 32. Critical fuel shortages also limited the number of sorties that could be flown.

Nearly all available Fw 190 fighter-bomber units, including SG 1, SG 2, SG 3, SG 4, SG 10 and SG 77, had been transferred to the Eastern Front by September 1944, since it was recognised that the Soviets now presented an even greater threat than the Western Allies. With a last ditch effort the Soviets were temporarily held back, and a shaky front line was established along the River Vistula in Poland.

COURLAND POCKET

By mid-October, the Soviets had overrun the headquarters of the 3rd Panzer Army and advanced as far as the Baltic, cutting off what remained of Army Group North and Luftflotte 1 in northwest Latvia—an area that became known as the Courland pocket.

Among the units operating the Fw 190 in the area were II. and III./SG 3 in their ground-attack role, with the fighters of I. and II./JG 54 engaging Soviet single-seaters and bombers alike. Ferocious battles were fought over and around the pocket, with the two fighter Gruppen shooting down 31 enemy aircraft on 9 October alone.

The Russians tried repeatedly to crush the pocket throughout the month, and on 29 October they launched an attack with 1800 bombers and fighter-bombers. Even this seemingly overwhelming force failed to dislodge the well dug-in German ground forces, however. JG 54 continued to shoot down Il-2s, Pe-2s and Yak-9s, notably destroying 42 on 21 December 1944.

THE GREAT BLOW

On the Western Front, the German army had managed to halt the Allied advance by October, and the Luftwaffe was able to concentrate on the waves of heavy bombers regularly pounding German industry.

General der Jagdflieger Generalleutnant Adolf Galland used this opportunity to lay out plans for what he called 'the Great Blow'—an attack en masse that would inflict catastrophic damage during one of the Eighth Air Force's larger bombing raids. If half of

ABOVE: When the Allies overran Lechfeld on 29 April 1945, they found, among other aircraft, Fw 190 A-8 'White 40'.

ABOVE: The broken remains of Fw 190 'Black 3' lie abandoned. Hundreds of similar wrecks were collected up and scrapped at the end of the war, alongside pristine newly built examples and everything in between.

ABOVE: Clear-up crews had to drag wrecked Fw 190s out of the strangest places and situations after the war. Here a flock of sheep vie for a shady spot beneath the wreck of Fieseler-built Fw 190 A-8 W.Nr. 682989 in the vicinity of Nuremberg, Bavaria, in 1946.

the Americans had also built several pontoon bridges nearby.

By the middle of April the Soviets had a staggering 150 divisions massed along the Oder, supported by some 7500 combat aircraft of all types. The Luftwaffe had just over 2000 aircraft remaining and little fuel to put in them. The Russian attack on Berlin itself began on 16 April, and encirclement began on 24 April. Among the Fw 190 units defending the capital to the last were JG 3, I./SG 1 and II./SG 1.

When the Soviets finally took the city, those remaining Luftwaffe personnel with sufficient fuel left to fly their aircraft made a desperate attempt to fly westwards and surrender to the British and Americans. Others attempted to escape westwards on foot or by road vehicle. Still others had no choice but to surrender to the Russians. The Fw 190's service to the Third Reich was over.

Chapter 8

Special Weapons and Versions

FW 190 MISTEL

During 1942, work was carried out in Germany to enable a glider to carry a full military load by launching it into the air using a smaller-powered aircraft mounted on its back. This combination was eventually to become known as the Mistel (mistletoe) since the powered aircraft could be given an extended range using fuel drawn from the glider below—like mistletoe drawing sap from its host tree.

The upper portion was to be a Bf 109 E fighter, the lower a DFS 230 glider. Both were piloted.

In June 1943, it was decided that this technology could be used for launching a 'grossbombe' or large bomb at a ground target. The Bf 109 would still be the upper portion, now a 109 F, but the lower would be a 'war-weary' unmanned Junkers Ju 88 A-4 containing 3.5 tons of explosives.

The Bf 109 pilot would control the whole Mistel up to its arrival over the target, whereupon the Ju 88 would be aimed and an autopilot unit within it activated. The Bf 109 would separate from the Ju 88 by firing explosive bolts and then peel away as the bomb flew down to its target.

The Ju 88's warhead was a huge hollow charge with a plunger detonator that was fitted in place of the aircraft's cockpit. They were to be used against high-value targets such as capital ships, power stations or bridges.

Junkers and the DFS worked together on the project, code-named Beethoven-Gerät or Beethoven Device, and by April 1944 production of the first batch of 15 Mistel was under way. The first unit to operate them, 2./KG 101, was ready for action in June.

By the end of November a new version of the Mistel combination, with an Fw 190 as the upper component, was being tested. Unfortunately, the Ju 88 A-4 used 87-octane fuel, whereas the Fw 190 A used 95 octane—making them incompatible. The solution was to pair either an Fw 190 A-8 or F-8 with a Ju 88 G-1 night fighter airframe, which also used 95-octane fuel.

Plans to convert 75 G-1s for use as the 'Mistel 2' were laid out on 5 December 1944, and 12 were ready by 21 December. Deliveries to the unit intended to operate them, 6./KG 200, began at the end of December. Production was slowed, however, by a shortage of 'donor' Ju 88 G-1s, so on 6 January night fighter unit I./NJG 4 was ordered to hand over 43 of its G-1s for Mistel 2 conversion by 15 January.

With the Allies now advancing from the west and the Soviets from the east, it was difficult for II./KG 200 to find a suitably large stationary target for its Mistels to attack. Göring came up with the answer—the Royal Navy's

Home Fleet at Scapa Flow. This idea rapidly coalesced into a solid plan—Unternehmen Drachenhöhle or Operation Dragon's Lair.

Fifteen Mistel 2s from 6./KG 200 would form the strike force, supported by 12 flare-dropping Ju 88s and 188s from 5./KG 200 to illuminate the target. They were to set off from Tirstrup, in Denmark, in late January 1945. Everything initially went according to plan, and II./KG 200's Mistels and Ju 88/188s arrived at Tirstrup in mid-January 1945, but bad weather prevented the attack from going ahead.

On 3 February four Mistel 1s were send to Tirstrup to bolster the attack force but were shot down by American Mustangs. Eleven days later, a pair of de Havilland Mosquito Mk.VIs from the Royal Air Force's (RAF's) Fighter Experimental Flight attacked Tirstrup. Two of the Mistel combinations were destroyed, and Operation Dragon's Lair was cancelled.

While the pilots of 6./KG 200 had been awaiting the green light, another Mistel operation had been planned—Operation Eisenhammer or 'Iron Hammer'. This was to be an attack on 23 hydro-electric and steam power stations around Moscow with the intention of crippling Soviet manufacturing capability. It was to be carried out by pilots of 3./KG(J) 30 from Peenemünde under the supervision of KG 200.

ABOVE: A camouflaged Mistel 2, probably belonging to II./KG(J) 30 and based at Oranienburg in March 1945. The Ju 88 G-1's warhead has an unusual short SHL 3500 fuse and both component aircraft carry a drop tank – probably in readiness for participation in Operation Iron Hammer.

Even as pilot training and briefings were being given, the Soviet Army advanced to within striking distance of Berlin, and on 30 March 1945, Eisenhammer was put on hold. Eleven days later, 18 Mistel intended for the operation were destroyed during a US bombing raid on Rechlin-Lärz. Another five were destroyed at Oranienburg.

On Sunday, 25 March 1945, four 6./KG 200 Mistel took off from Burg to attack US forces erecting pontoon bridges over the River Rhine near Oppenheim.

Leutnant Fred Lew, who took part in the mission, said:

"Following a wide left turn, our formation headed towards the Rhine. Initially, we were at 1500m but soon climbed to a cruising altitude of 2000m. The approach flight took two and a half hours. As it began to turn dark, so I saw the River Rhine glittering below us in the moonlight.

"Meanwhile, our Beleuchter aircraft had dropped their signal flares, but still, I could not recognise the bridge. I flew a full circle to orientate myself, but as I did so, I ran into heavy American anti-aircraft fire. In order to locate the target I descended to 1500m and then – bang! I was hit. My Mistel lurched to port and went into a spin on its back. As I was no longer able to control the machine, I decided to separate my Fw 190 while simultaneously diving away from the Mistel.

"At 300-400m, I finally managed to regain control over my aircraft and got away from that terrible flak and headed east towards Burg. In the darkness and flying on instruments, my return flight became quite hairy and I flew off course. I found myself approaching the River Elbe. Since the Russians were by now quite close, it was dangerous to cross the river.

"Fortunately, I reached the Elbe at Torgau. The success of the operation was virtually nil."

The last significant Mistel operations came in mid- to late April 1945. On 11 April, Mistel had been used to attack autobahn bridges crossing the Kwisa and Bóbr rivers to stem the Russian advance. On 12 April four Mistel from 6./KG 200 and four from KG(J) 30 had been ordered to attack bridges at Küstrin—a town in Brandenbrug, East Prussia, that straddled the River Oder.

It had been designated a 'fortress' by Hitler, but Soviet forces had succeeded in annihilating its German defenders by 11 March and were using its bridges to bring thousands of men and machines over the river.

All eight Mistel were gathered at Peenemünde and set off in two waves. The 6./KG 200 aircraft went first in the morning and began, one by one, to take off. The first combination had a problem, however, and although the Fw 190 separated cleanly, the Ju 88 rolled over and crashed into the Baltic. The second suffered a burst left tyre and crashed. One took off, but the fourth also failed. Just one Mistel was left to see the mission through, and the pilot was Rudi Riedl.

He met up with his fighter escort—a single Bf 109—and they flew to Küstrin together.

"Nearer the target he flew close to me and, with his thumb, pointed downwards at my target. We must have crossed the front line then, because all hell broke loose. I was so surprised. After all, this was my first operational sortie. The target lay before me ringed by a hail of fire.

"As I made my attack dive, my fighter escort climbed away to stay beyond the range of the enemy flak. All I could see around me were black clouds from the flak. Occasionally, as well as these black clouds, I could see little flashes of light from the tracer – just like when you throw more wood onto an already burning fire.

"I don't actually remember pressing the button to activate the separation, but my diving speed was 600-650km/h. The lower component hit the first section of the three section bridge which exploded and landed on top of the next section."

During the attack, Riedl's Fw 190 suffered a buckled wing, but he eventually managed to land at Strausberg.

ABOVE: The first operational Mistel combination utilised a Bf 109 F, in this case WNr. 10130, paired with a Ju 88 A-4, WNr. 10096.

The second wave from KG(J) 30 all took off successfully in the afternoon, led by a Ju 88 of I./KG 66. They reached the target, and all four Ju 88s were reportedly launched at the Küstrin bridges, but none of them caused any significant damage.

On 14 April, another three Mistel from I./KG(J) 30 took off to attack the Küstrin bridges, and five Mistel from unidentified units launched an attack on bridges at Görlitz over the Lusatian Neisse River. The success or failure of this operation is unknown.

16 April saw four Mistel from 6./KG 200 ordered to make yet another attempt at the Küstrin bridges, but this time, as they took off, they were intercepted by Allied fighters. Two were shot down, but the others reached the bridges, and one Mistel destroyed a bridge. The following day, seven more Mistel were prepared for another Küstrin attack, but one crashed on take-off and the rest were grounded.

Another Mistel attack on the Küstrin bridges was launched on 27 April and another on bridges over the Oder between Tantow and Greifenhagen on 30 April. Neither was successful, and thereafter Mistel operations were ended.

Other Mistel using the Fw 190 were planned. Had the twin-engined Focke-Wulf Ta 154 fighter entered into full production, it was to have formed the lower part of a Mistel combination for use against bomber formations. It would have been radio controlled, rather than being guided by an autopilot system.

The Mistel 3 combination also used the Fw 190 but paired with a Ju 88 G-1. The Mistel 3A was a training version, matching an Fw 190 A-8 or F-8 to a standard Ju 88 A-4, while the Mistel 3B involved matching an A-8 with a long-range Ju 88 H-4 heavy fighter. The Fw 190 A-8 was to be fitted with Doppelreiter streamlined fuel tanks above its wings for

ABOVE: A Mistel S3C trainer combination on the runway at Junkers' Bernberg factory. The aircraft in the foreground clearly shows the stretched fuselage of the Ju 88 G-10.

increased range. The Mistel 3C paired an Fw 190 F-8 with a Ju 88 G-10.

A smaller Mistel was also planned, which involved an Fw 190 sitting atop a Fieseler Fi 103 'V-1' flying bomb.

RUHRSTAHL/KRAMER X-4 MISSILE

Development work on the X-4 wire-guided air-to-air missile began in July 1943, and it was intended for use by both the Fw 190 and the Me 262. It was powered by a BMW 109-548 liquid-fuelled rocket engine and had wooden fins with fairings at their tips containing 8.5km of fine wire on bobbins for the guidance system. The 20-kg warhead was effective to about 8m.

The first tests, using converted F-8 Fw 190 V69, WNr. 582072, took place on 11 August 1944, at E-Stelle Tarnewitz on the Baltic coast. An X-4 was fitted beneath each wing on an ETC 71 rack. Four more Fw 190s were also used in tests—V70 and a trio of F-8s.

When the missile was launched, the pilot had to manually guide it to its target, using a joystick mounted on the instrument panel. This was difficult, however, and development moved onto aircraft with two or more crew such as the Ju 88. In the end, although 1000-1300 X-4s were built, their engines were destroyed when BMW's factory at Stargard was bombed.

RHEINMETALL-BORSIG RZ 65 FÖHN ROCKET

Fw 190 V69 was used to test another weapon, the Föhn or 'Warm Wind' rocket. This solid fuel rocket was unguided and was launched from short tubes that could be mounted

ABOVE: One of a pair of Mistel S2s captured by the Americans at Junkers' Merseburg facility in May 1945. The upper portion is an Fw 190 A-8, and the Ju 88 is a G-1, WNr. 590153.

ABOVE: The wire-guided X-4 air-to-air missile was intended for use by high-performance fighters such as the Fw 190 and Me 262, but although more than 1000 were made, all of the rocket engines intended for the type were destroyed in a bombing raid before they could be delivered.

singly or in groups either beneath the host aircraft's wings or, in the case of V69, within them.

Tests offered promising results, but the weapon never saw active service.

R4M ORKAN

The Rakete 4kg Minenkopf (R4M) or Rocket 4kg Explosive warhead was designed as an air-to-air unguided rocket for use against bomber formations. Thirteen could be mounted beneath each wing of an Fw 190 and could be fired in four salvos of six or seven. They could be extremely effective and were used in active service, but most were diverted to Me 262 units.

SG 113 FÖRSTERSONDE

The Förstersonde or 'Forest Probe' was an anti-tank weapon fitted vertically within the wings of its carrier aircraft. Its 45-mm shells were automatically fired straight downwards via a system that detected alterations in the earth's magnetic field caused by heavy armoured vehicles. The idea was to fly the Fw 190 in either a shallow dive or horizontally at low level above an enemy armoured formation, and the weapon would do the rest. Tests using Fw 190 V75 and a pair of F-8s showed, however, that the weapon was a little too effective. When it destroyed a tank, the resulting explosion was likely to also destroy the attacking aircraft.

SG 116 ZELLENDUSCHE

The SG 116 Zellendusche or 'Airframe shower' system was a series of fuselage-mounted upward pointing tubes, each containing a single MK 103 30-mm shell. The idea was for the Fw 190 pilot to fly beneath a bomber formation, and a photo-electric cell would fire the weapon automatically when a bomber's shadow passed across it. Two F-8s tested the weapon on a Heinkel He 177, but the results were unimpressive.

SG 117 ROHRBLOCK

The Rohrblock or 'Tube block' was similar to the SG 116, but the seven tubes were arranged in a cluster and contained MK 108 shells. It

ABOVE: The RZ 65 rocket launcher tubes fitted into the wing structure of Fw 190 V69 appear as three holes in the leading edge of each wing.

ABOVE: The SG 113 weapons system was carried vertically within each wing of the Fw 190. It was fired downwards automatically when passing over a tank. The attacking pilot had to be flying low for it to work but so low that the blast resulting from the tank being blown up stood a good chance of destroying the aircraft too.

was intended that a pair of 'Rohrblocks' would be fitted aft of the Fw 190's cockpit. Tests were carried out using Fw 190 V74.

BLOHM AND VOSS BV 246 HAGELKORN

Designed for use primarily with He 111s or Ju 88s, the Hagelkorn 'Hailstone' was an unpowered flying bomb that could glide to its target after airborne launch. It had a narrow streamlined fuselage and extremely narrow wings. It also had an electric gyroscopic guidance system, which made automatic corrections to the rudder to maintain its course. Further control was given via FuG 103 equipment carried within the launcher aircraft. Tests using four Fw 190s were carried out during the summer of 1944. It had been hoped that the Bv 246 could home in on radio transmitters in England and destroy them, but development was still incomplete when the war ended.

GERO II

Gero I had been a rearward firing flamethrower designed early in the war primarily to create a lot of smoke and thereby prevent enemy fighters from getting a clear shot at German bombers. This was abandoned, but the idea was revived in early 1945, with Soviet troops advancing rapidly into Germany, as an airborne flamethrower for attacking enemy infantry.

It was, essentially, a tank full of napalm-like fuel that could be attached to an Fw 190 F-8 via an ETC 504 fuselage rack. A nozzle would direct the ignited chemicals rearwards

ABOVE: The SG 116 was a series of tubes with MK 103 30mm cannon shells inside. When the carrier aircraft passed beneath a bomber it was designed to fire automatically. It practice, it was inaccurate and ineffective.

ABOVE: The long wings of the Blohm & Voss Bv 246 glider bomb are evident in this photo. It was designed to soar down onto its target guided by radio waves – either from the target itself or from the host aircraft.

and downwards onto the enemy. Three versions were designed, Gero IIA, IIB and IIC. The project never advanced to the prototype stage.

STRAHLJÄGER

The quest to find an alternative engine for the Fw 190 included the investigation of a jet solution. A T1 turbojet, designed in-house by Focke-Wulf, would have fitted right onto the Fw 190's nose. Thrust would initially come from all around the rear portion of the engine's cowling, except in front of the cockpit. This was later modified to nozzles venting along the centre of the fuselage beneath the aircraft. The design was set out in a Focke-Wulf document dated 5 November 1942, but performance figures were less than stellar, and the project was abandoned.

SWEPT OR GULL WING

A drawing produced by Focke-Wulf on 14 November 1941 shows a normal Fw 190 wing and then below it a wing sharply swept forward and then back. This is described on the drawing as the 'arrow wing', and Focke-Wulf appears to have pursued the idea further in 1942. A swept wing Fw 190 model, based on the Fw 190 V5g, was tested by the Aerodynamische Versuchsanstalt Göttingen, which then produced a report on the project on 21 January 1943.

DOPPELREITER FUEL TANKS

Extending the Fw 190's range was, like improving its armament, a constant concern of Focke-Wulf throughout the war years. Experiments were therefore carried out in-

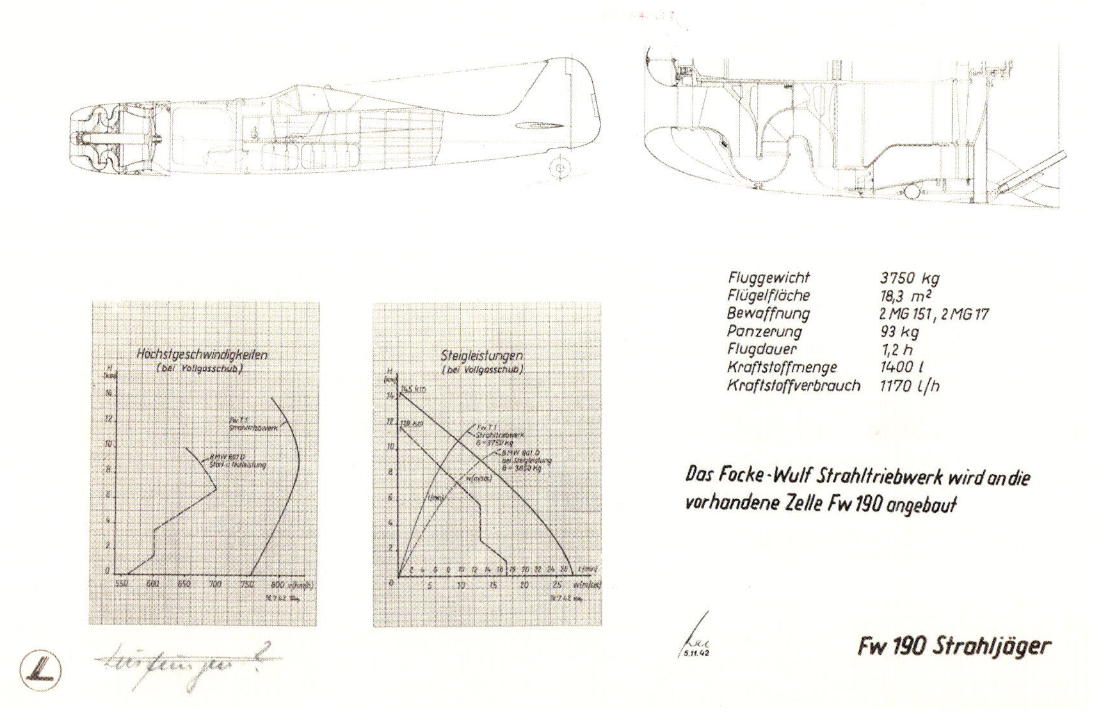

ABOVE: Focke-Wulf document from November 1942 showing the fitment and operation of the company's own T1 jet design to the Fw 190. Projected performance of other jet fighters, such as the Me 262, meant the jet Fw 190 was never taken forward.

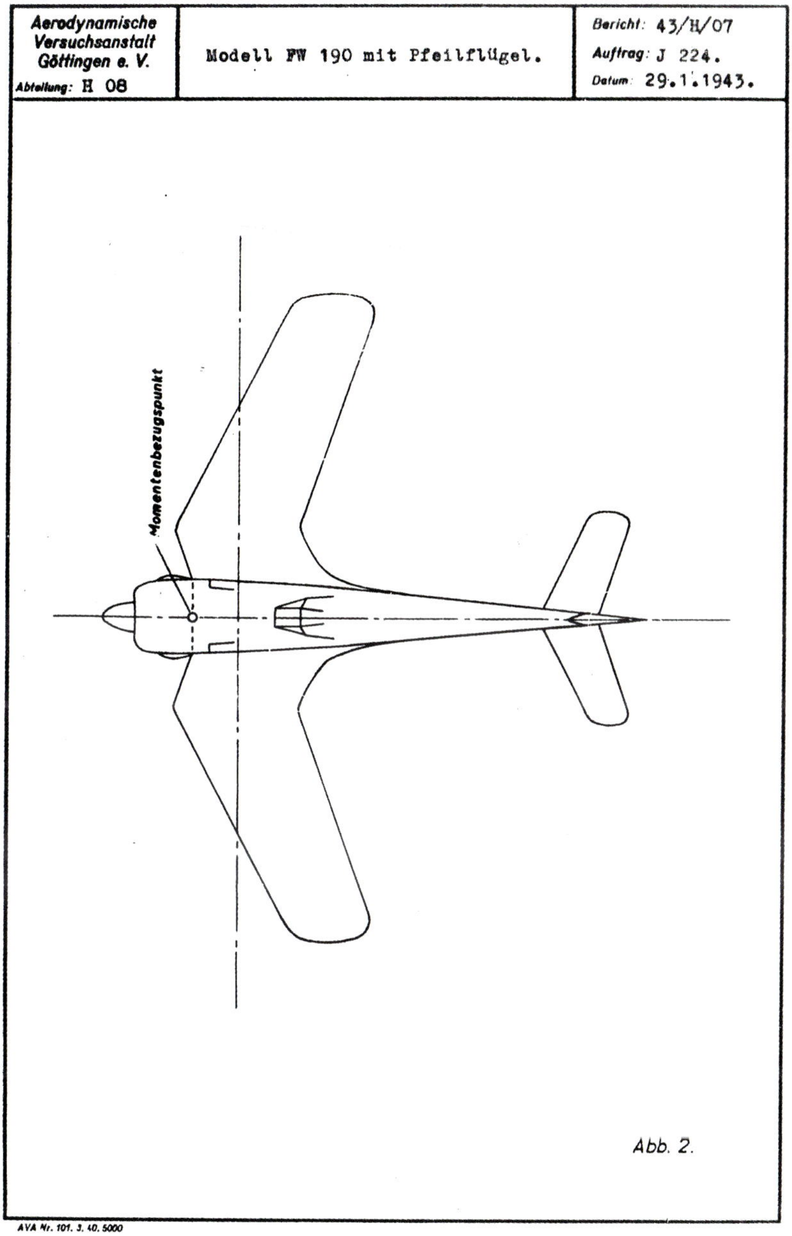

ABOVE: A drawing showing the swept wing Fw 190 model, based on the Fw 190 V5g, tested by the AVA in Göttingen. The idea seems to have been worked on from 1941 to the beginning of 1943.

volving a streamlined fuel tank mounted above each wing—where they would not interfere with weapons load or even additional drop tanks. Tests were carried out in July and August of 1944 using an Fw 190 A-8 and a G-2. A later design had the tanks built into the leading edges of the aircraft's wings, but neither type went into full production.

Umbau Mods and Rüstsatz Kits

This chapter gives details of the basic characteristics of the 10 Fw 190 A types manufactured, but for each type there were alternative versions produced, usually in small numbers or as one-offs, at the factory. These were indicated by a 'U' number, such as Fw 190 A-8/U1. Some only existed as proposals.

In addition, most of the Fw 190 A types were supported with Rüstsatz conversion kits that could be fitted in the field. When added to a standard aircraft, altering its characteristics, they were referred to in the type's designation using an 'R' number, such as Fw 190 A-4/R6.

Here are all the Fw 190 A Umbau modifications and Rüstsatz kits. Where a number is missing, e.g. Fw 190 A-4/R3, either that designation was never allocated or it is simply unknown to what it may have referred.

FW 190 A-0

A-0/U1—Armament of 4 × MG 17, two in wing roots and two above the engine.

A-0/U2—Armament of 2 × MG 17 above the engine, 2 × MG 131 in wing roots.

A-0/U3—Fitted with FuG 25 radio equipment.

A-0/U4—Fitted with 300-litre drop tank.

A-0/U5—Armament of 2 × MG 17 above the engine, 2 × MG 151 in wing roots.

A-0/U6—Fitted with American Wright Cyclone engine. Proposal only.

A-0/U7—Fitted with early BMW 801 D engine.

A-0/U8—Fitted with composite BMW 801 C/D engine.

A-0/U9—Fitted with BMW 801 C-1 but work abandoned.

A-0/U10—Armament of 2 × MG 17 above the engine, 2 × MG 151 in wing roots, 2 × MG FF-C2 in outer wings.

A-0/U11—BMW 801 C-1 fitted in place of BMW 801 C-0. New undercarriage design.

A-0/U12—Fitted with BMW 801 C-1 with GM-1 nitrous oxide injection.

FW 190 A-1

A-1/U1—BMW 801 D test machine.

FW 190 A-2

A-2/U1—Fitted with Patin PKS 11 directional control, a form of autopilot.

A-2/U3—Reconnaissance version fitted with 2 × Rb 12.5/7 × 9s camera in fuselage. EK 16 Robot camera fitted in port wing leading edge.

A-2/Sk—Fitted with Heine ski undercarriage.

FW 190 A-3

A-3/U1—Test frame for nose extension standardised in A-5.

A-3/U2—Six RZ 65 73mm air-to-air rocket tubes fitted in outer wing positions.

A-3/U3—Reconnaissance version with two Rb 12.5/7 × 9 cameras in fuselage behind pilot's seat.

A-3/U3 (later version)—Ground-attack aircraft with extra armour on nose and on undercarriage doors. Various armament combinations tried. 12 built.

A-3/U4—Reconnaissance version with 1 × Rb 20/30, Rb 50/30 or Rb 75/30 or 2 × Rb

12.5/7 × 9. Robot camera in port wing leading edge and FuG 17 army radio also fitted. Fittings to carry 2 × 300 litre drop tanks or 8 × 110lb SC 50 bombs. Twelve built.

A-3/U5—High-altitude version. Reduced weight, no armour, armament reduced to 2 × MG 151 in wing roots. Engine moved 6in forward. Proposal only.

A-3/U6—As U5 except with pilot's seat armoured and without engine move. Proposal only.

A-3/U7—BMW 801 D-2 without management system, armament reduced to 2 × MG 151 in wing roots. External air intakes on engine cowling. Three built, redesignated as A-4/U7 and served with Stab./JG 2.

A-3 tp—Tropical filters fitted.

Aa-3—Export version for Turkey. Armament of 2 × MG 17 in wing roots, 2 × MG FF in outer wing positions. FuG 25 radio removed. 70 built.

FW 190 A-4

A-4/U1—Fitted with BMW 801 C-2 engine.

A-4/U3—Ground-attack aircraft with extra armour on nose and on undercarriage doors. Various armament combinations. Developed as Fw 190 F-1.

A-4/U4—Reconnaissance version similar to A-3/U4.

A-5/U5—High-altitude version similar to A-3/U5. Proposal only.

A-5/U6—Similar to A-3/U6. Proposal only.

A-4/U7—Redesignation of A-3/U7.

A-4/U8—Fighter-bomber version. Provision for 300-litre drop tank, 1 × 500kg SC500 bomb, 1 × AB 500 weapon container, 1 × 250kg SC250 bomb or 4 × 50kg SC50 bombs under fuselage. Fittings for wing loads of 2 × SC250 or 4 × SC50. Eventually produced as Fw 190 G-1.

A-4/R1—Fitted with FuG 16 ZE radio to act as formation leader.

A-4/R6—Fitted with 2 × WGr 21 mortar tubes, one under each wing.

A-4 tp—Tropical filters fitted.

FW 190 A-5

A-5/U1—Fitted with BMW 801 C-2 engine. One only.

A-5/U2—Armament reduced to 2 × MG 151. 3 × 300-litre drop tanks. Flame-dampers fitted around fuselage. Double searchlight in port wing. Four built. Developed into Fw 190 G-3/N long-range night fighter-bomber.

A-5/U3—Two ETC 50 bomb racks under each wing. Extra armour fitted. Originally intended to enter full production as A-6 fighter-bomber but redesignated F-2 instead. A-5/U3 tp had tropical filters.

A-5/U4—Reconnaissance version similar to A-3/U4. Initially called A-7, then changed to Fw 190 E-1, but no serial production followed.

A-5/U4 tp—A-5/U4 fitted with tropical filters.

A-5/U8—Fighter-bomber version with Messerschmitt designed wing racks and Robot camera in port wing. Developed into Fw 190 G-2.

A-5/U9—Larger wings (10.5m span) and armament changed to 4 × MG 151 in wings and 2 × MG 131 on nose.

A-5/U10—MG FF cannon in outer wings replaced with MG 151/20.

A-5/U11—1 × podded MK 103 cannon under each wing outboard of landing gear. Developed into R3 conversion kit for A-6, A-8, F-3 and F-8.

A-5/U12—2 × podded MG 151/20 cannon under each wing. Developed into A-6/R1.

A-5/U13—Fighter-bomber version similar to A-5/U8 but with fittings for 1 × SC250 under each wing. Directional control fitted, balloon cable cutter and Robot camera. Developed as the Fw 190 G-3.

A-5/U14—Torpedo carrier. Fitted with modified ETC rack to carry 1 × LTF 5b torpedo. Modified flaps, enlarged vertical tail surfaces, extended tailwheel leg. Armament reduced to 2 × MG 151/20.

A-5/U15—Torpedo carrier similar to A-5/U14 but with autopilot, target finder and fittings for one drop tank under each wing. Increased armour.

A-5/U16—1 × MK 108 cannon in each outer wing position. Developed into A-6/R2.

A-5/U17—Ground-attack version. Extra armour. Outer wing MG FFs swapped for MG 151/20s. ETC 501 rack under fuselage and each wing. Developed into Fw 190 F-3/R1.

A-5/U18—MW 50 water methanol injection for BMW 801.

A-5/R1—Similar to A-4/R1 but based on A-5.

A-5/R6—Similar to A-4/R6 but based on A-5.

A-5 trop—Tropical filters fitted.

FW 190 A-6

A-6/R1—As per A-5/U12.

A-6/R2—As per A-5/U16 but based on A-6 airframe.

A-6/R3—As per A-5/U11.

A-6/R4—BMW 801 D-2 fitted with GM-1 nitrous oxide injection.

A-6/R6—As per A-4/R6 but based on A-6 airframe.

A-6 tp—Tropical filters fitted.

FW 190 A-7

A-7/R1—2 × MG 151/20 in a pod under each wing. Proposal only.

A-7/R2—As per A-5/U16 but based on A-7 airframe.

A-7/R3—1 × MK 103 in a pod under each wing, replacing MG 151. Proposal only.

A-7/R6—As per A-4/R6 but based on A-7 airframe.

FW 190 A-8

A-8/U1—Two-seat trainer version, also known as the Fw 190 S-8.

A-8/U2 –Fitting of TSA 2 bombsight. Proposal only.

A-8/R1—2 × MG 151/20 in a pod under each wing. Proposal only.

A-8/R2—As per A-5/U16 but based on A-8 airframe.

A-8/R3—1 × MK 103 in a pod under each wing, replacing MG 151.

A-8/R4—As per A-8/R3 but with the MK 103 inside the wing rather than under it.

A-8/R5—Fitted with 115-litre fuselage tank. Proposal dropped when this became standard fit for the A-8.

A-8/R6—As per A-4/R6 but based on A-8 airframe.

A-8/R7—Extra armour but retaining standard A-8 armament. Proposal only.

A-8/R8—Extra armour. Armament altered to MK 108s in outer wing positions.

A-8/R11—Bad weather fighter with BMW 801 TU engine, Patin PKS 12 autopilot, heated windscreen and port side canopy to reduce condensation, EZ 42 gunsight, Lorenz FuG 125 Hermine radio.

A-8/R12—As per A-8/R11 but with A-5/U16 armament.

FW 190 A-9

A-9/U3—The A-9 as the upper portion of a Mistel combination, with the lower part being a Ta 154.

A-9/R1—2 × MG/151 under each wing.

A-9/R2—2 × MK 108 in the outer wing positions.

A-9/R3—1 × MK 103 under each wing.

A-9/R6—As per A-4/R6 but based on A-9 airframe.

A-9/R8—As per A-8/R8 but based on A-9 airframe.

A-9/R11—As per A-8/R11. Significant number of this variant produced.

A-9/R12—As per A-8/R11 but with A-9/R2 armament fitted.